Acing
Criminal Law

Fifth Edition

A Checklist Approach to Criminal Law

John M. Burkoff
Professor of Law Emeritus
University of Pittsburgh
School of Law

Series Editor
A. Benjamin Spencer

ACING SERIES®

WEST ACADEMIC PUBLISHING

860 Blue Gentian Road, Suite 350
Eagan, MN 55121
1-877-888-1330

Printed in the United States of America

ISBN: 979-8-88786-282-8

To Nancy, Amy & Sean, David & Emmy, and Emma, Molly, Hannah, and Cyrus, with love.
JMB

Acknowledgments

The author wishes to thank Professor Cynthia Lee, Edward F. Howrey Professor of Law, George Washington University Law School, for her extremely helpful comments on some of the material contained in an earlier edition of Acing Criminal Law.

Introduction

Most students spend a good deal of time developing an outline for each course—a lengthy (sometimes well over 100 pages) and exhaustive document that purports to compile the universe of information presented in a course into an organized, accessible format that is meant to simplify studying and provide a useful source for information during the exam (provided the exam is open-book).

Unfortunately, personal outlines often do no more than provide a restatement of various principles of law or doctrine organized by topic. It remains for you to take those doctrines and apply them to the fact patterns presented on exams. That process of applying legal principles to facts is a large part of what exams and lawyering are all about; knowing the relevant law is only half (oftentimes less than half) of the battle. So why are you and your fellow students devoting all of this time and energy into developing these miniature volumes on the course material and not putting more energy into developing a tool that could help guide your legal analysis or problems presented on exams?

In addition to an outline, there is another document that some students occasionally develop as an examination aid: a checklist. There is no single definition for a checklist or a consistent approach to drafting one. But a checklist is meant to present in a sparse and simplified way the basics about a topic that you want to be sure to remember to discuss or evaluate in the course of your examination answer. Some checklists are simply elements or rules under larger topical headings. Others are more involved in linking various concepts together in a logical pattern that facilitates the analysis of legal problems. Regardless of the format, most checklists do not make much of a contribution beyond being a condensed form of the lengthier outline prepared for the course.

Properly conceived and crafted, however, checklists can fulfill the role of providing a tool that truly aids you in your effort to analyze legal problems in your courses. There is a general structure to legal analysis that involves identifying the issue, articulating the applicable legal rules and principles, applying those principles to a given set of facts, and then arriving at and stating a conclusion. A checklist is the document that organizes a collection of rules, identifying all of the relevant questions and issues that you should consider in order to completely analyze a question.

The purpose of this book is to present you with a comprehensive set of checklists pertaining to each of the topics typically covered in a substantive criminal law course. The checklists are meant to provide you with a tool that facilitates the analysis of criminal law problems. Each chapter focuses on a different topic, typical and illustrative exam-type problems are posed and analyzed to illustrate just how the checklists can be used to resolve such problems. Each chapter concludes with a section entitled "Points to Remember" to recapitulate key points that you need to remember when answering exam questions. A concluding chapter provides some final thoughts on preparing for and taking exams generally. At the end of the book there is an Appendix that presents condensed "mini-checklists" for each topic. You may find these useful during the time crunch of an exam when you need quick access to the full range of major concepts that are pertinent to an issue.

You should use this book to assist yourself in developing your own analytical process for addressing and answering the questions you will face on your examinations. The steps outlined in the checklists presented here can provide you with a map for how you should proceed when evaluating any given legal issue relating to criminal law. Funneling your analysis through the checklist will also improve the chances that your answer will fully display a reasoned analysis while also arriving at a sound conclusion. But these checklists can only be used effectively if you have a thorough understanding of the substantive material.

This book does not attempt to explain substantive criminal law rules and doctrines in any great detail; rather, it seeks merely to organize these rules and doctrines into a dynamic tool that you can use to apply legal principles to typical fact patterns that you might face on exams. You should, of course, use these checklists in conjunction with your own course materials, particularly your class notes and your outlines, to prepare for your exams. Use of these checklists should enhance your ability to write reasoned and sound responses to examination questions. Further, these checklists should be helpful in putting the course material in perspective and providing a clearer picture of how the concepts you are learning should be integrated into a legal analysis. Finally, you should make sure to modify these checklists according to the areas of emphasis and coverage of your professor.

So, what are you waiting for? Get out there and ace Criminal Law!

Table of Contents

Acing
Criminal Law
Fifth Edition

CHAPTER 1

Nature of Criminal Law

A. IN GENERAL

Common law roots vs. statutes. In the early American colonies and even after the American Revolution ended, each of the states in the United States "borrowed" its criminal laws from the English Common Law. English common law crimes included such classic offenses as murder, manslaughter, mayhem, rape, larceny, robbery, burglary, arson, assault, battery, perjury, forgery, bribery, and conspiracy. Today, however, most states long ago repealed this common law of crimes. But even where that has not occurred formally, criminal statutes specifically defining the elements of offenses—some of them similar to the old common law crimes, but most of them newer and different—have largely supplanted these common law crimes as the primary basis for criminal punishment.

Crimes Codes. Every state, as well as the federal government, now has literally thousands of statutory provisions on the books that contain criminal penalties. Some of these jurisdictions have special, discrete sections of their statutes that deal specifically with criminal offenses, and these are often called "Crimes Codes." Still other jurisdictions, like the federal, do not have a Crimes Code at all, but instead have thousands of criminal provisions scattered throughout all of the various statutory titles.

Categories of crimes. Most jurisdictions distinguish between crimes that are classified as "felonies" and crimes that are classified as "misdemeanors." Felonies are the most serious offenses, and are typically subject to a potential sentence of 1 year or more in prison. Misdemeanors are less serious offenses, and are typically punished by a fine and/or a potential sentence of less than 1 year in jail. *Lange v. California,* 141 S. Ct. 2011, 2020 (2021) ("A 'felon' is not always 'more dangerous than a misdemeanant,' but calling an offense a misdemeanor usually limits prison time to one year."). Some jurisdictions also possess an even lower category of very minor crimes, often called summary offenses, violation of which will not result in any incarceration at all.

Model Penal Code. In 1962, the American Law Institute adopted a model Crimes Code called the Model Penal Code (MPC). The MPC provisions are not good law in and of themselves. Indeed, some provisions were never adopted by any state, and others are outdated by now. But many states have enacted significant portions of the MPC as a part of their own Crimes Codes, and many courts continue to refer to MPC provisions and commentary in interpreting criminal statutes. As a result, the MPC remains an important reference point for understanding criminal law in the United States.

Jury trials. The Sixth Amendment to the U.S. Constitution establishes a right to a jury trial. The Supreme Court has interpreted this language to apply to all criminal charges where an accused faces potential imprisonment of more than six months. Accordingly, many criminal trials are jury trials. When that happens, the jury finds the facts. Where, however, the right to a jury trial is waived or is otherwise inapplicable, the trial judge rules on applicable law and is also the fact-finder. This is called a "bench trial."

Proving crimes. Each criminal offense consists of a unique set of distinct facts that must be proved, which are called "elements." The prosecution must prove each of these elements beyond a reasonable doubt in order to convict an accused person of the commission of that particular offense. The defense, in contrast, usually seeks to create a reasonable doubt about the existence of one or more of these elements in order to gain an acquittal. In addition, each jurisdiction also possesses some "affirmative defenses" that an accused may seek to use in his or her defense. *See* Chapters 14 (Justification Defenses) & 15 (Excuses).

Criminal vs. civil law. The criminal law is not concerned primarily with ensuring appropriate financial compensation to wronged parties, as the civil law is. Granted, it's true that convicted criminal defendants may have to pay large fines as a result of their criminal convictions, not unlike the economic damages that losing defendants in civil lawsuits may be obligated to pay. But, unlike the impact of the civil law, individuals who face criminal punishment must endure additionally the stigma and humiliation of criminal conviction and the very real possibility of forcible incarceration. The question naturally arises then: when and why is someone held to have committed a *crime* rather than simply an *unlawful* act, a civil wrong?

B. JUSTIFICATIONS FOR CRIMINAL PUNISHMENT

The primary rationales for the imposition of criminal punishment are: general deterrence; specific deterrence; incapacitation; rehabilitation; retribution; and the expression of community values. *See also, e.g., Holguin-Hernandez v. U.S.*, 140 S. Ct. 762, 765–66 (2020) ("Congress has instructed sentencing courts to impose sentences that are ' " sufficient, but not greater than necessary, to comply with" ' (among other things) certain basic objectives, including the need for 'just punishment, deterrence, protection of the public, and rehabilitation.' ").

General deterrence. As a basis for the justification of criminal punishment, general deterrence is the belief that by punishing people criminally for particular activity, other people will be deterred from engaging in that activity in the future. Many people question, however, how effective criminal statutes really are in deterring people from committing crimes. Are people really paying attention? Are these statutes really enforced with sufficient certainty and severity to serve as effective deterrents?

Specific deterrence. Specific deterrence is the belief that by punishing a particular person criminally, he or she will be deterred from committing that crime in the future. Given the high recidivism (repeat offender) rates for many crimes, there is some question whether specific deterrence is a truly effective justification for punishment.

Incapacitation. Incapacitation (sometimes called "restraint") is the simple recognition that putting someone in prison will keep that person from doing any further harm, at least outside the prison walls. The moral question remains, however: for what offenses should we put people in prison? And for how long?

Rehabilitation. Rehabilitation is the belief that a person convicted of a crime can be "cured" while incarcerated or under official supervision. It is an open question, however, whether we have rehabilitated in fact many or most of the convicted defendants who have been sent to prison. *See, e.g., Tapia v. U.S.*, 564 U.S. 319 (2011). Indeed, it is also questionable in some cases whether it is even possible to rehabilitate some categories of criminals. We have great difficulty, for example, rehabilitating convicted sex offenders.

Retribution. Retribution is the belief that we should punish a convicted criminal severely in order to give him just what he deserves for his conduct and/or simply as a matter of righteous vengeance. The fact that we can punish people retributively does not, of course, mean that we should. Unsurprisingly, some commentators have argued that criminal punishment that is only retributive—without any other justification—is inherently cruel and inappropriate. But the Supreme Court has nonetheless concluded that "[r]etribution is a legitimate reason to punish." *See, e.g., Graham v. Florida,* 560 U.S. 48, 71 (2010). *See also, e.g., Hall v. Florida,* 572 U.S. 701 (2014).

Expression of community values. The expression of community values as a basis for criminal punishment means that we punish certain conduct criminally in order to express our strong feelings about the wrongfulness of that conduct in order to educate and create a sense of community about what is morally right and wrong.

Application of justifications. Legislators often use one or more of these justifications for punishment as the basis for their decision whether or not and/or how severely to criminalize conduct in new legislation. In addition, sentencing judges often consider these very same justifications in exercising any sentencing discretion they may have, e.g. in deciding whether or not to impose a prison sentence at all, or if so, for how long.

The Supreme Court has held, furthermore, that imposition of the death penalty is constitutional as it can be based reasonably if not inevitably upon retributive or general deterrent justifications. *Gregg v. Georgia,* 428 U.S. 153 (1976). Such punishment has also been held not to be unconstitutionally "cruel and unusual." *Nance v. Ward,* 142 S. Ct. 2214 (2022); *Bucklew v. Precythe,* 139 S. Ct. 1112 (2019). However, by 2023, only 28 jurisdictions (27 states and the federal) still retain use of the death penalty.

NATURE OF CRIMINAL LAW CHECKLIST

A. **The Basics**—the criminal law was but is no longer based upon the English Common Law.

   1. **Statutes**—every jurisdiction has its own criminal statutes defining the elements of crimes.

   2. **Codes**—some jurisdictions have Crimes Codes and some (e.g. federal) do not.

   3. **Classification of Crimes**—felonies are more serious crimes than misdemeanors.

   4. **Model Penal Code**—many provisions adopted in Crimes Codes and referenced in court decisions.

5. **Proving Crimes**—each element of a crime must be proved by the prosecution beyond a reasonable doubt.

B. **Justifications for Punishment**—often used to determine what activity is criminalized and, if so, how severe the punishment can or will be.

1. **General Deterrence**—criminal punishments deter *other* people from committing that act.
2. **Specific Deterrence**—criminal punishment deters the actor from committing that act again.
3. **Incapacitation**—incarceration keeps people from committing crimes.
4. **Rehabilitation**—people can be "cured" of their criminal tendencies.
5. **Retribution**—just deserts and vengeance justify criminal punishment.
6. **Expression of Community Values**—criminal punishment educates people about what is wrong.

C. **Capital Punishment**—the Supreme Court has held the death penalty constitutional on the basis of retribution and general deterrence and not "cruel and unusual," but some states don't use it.

ILLUSTRATIVE PROBLEMS

These two problems illustrate two of the ways in which the justifications for punishment impact upon the decision to criminalize conduct and the severity of criminal sentences.

■ PROBLEM 1.1 ■

You are a legislative aide to a state legislator who is trying to decide whether or not to introduce a bill seeking to criminalize the use of mobile phones by individuals while they are riding on public transportation. Aside from the merits of such a proposal as a matter of reasoned public policy, what advice can you give your boss relating to whether or not such conduct should actually be made *a crime*?

Analysis

You need to analyze for your legislator employer whether the justifications for criminal punishment apply to a setting like this one and, if so, how they apply.

As to general deterrence, would the criminalization of the use of mobile phones on public transportation actually work to deter people generally from committing that act? That is an issue that needs to be addressed. Wouldn't the answer to that question depend, at least in part, on the nature of the proscribed conduct balanced against the *severity* of the criminal penalties prescribed, e.g. a $5 fine (not very deterrent) as opposed to 30 days in jail (very deterrent)?

Wouldn't general deterrence depend as well on the *certainty* (or lack thereof) that people would actually be arrested for this offense . . . and prosecuted and convicted? And wouldn't deterrence turn, further, on individuals' perceived need and/or desire to use their mobile phones in this venue, e.g. what if they wanted to use the phone to report an emergency such as someone apparently suffering a heart attack or to call their children because they were going to be home late?

Of course, even if strict and certain criminal penalties might have a discernible general deterrent effect, that does not mean necessarily that it is good public policy to enact criminal laws like these. That's a totally different question. The use of the death penalty to punish people who smoke in public buildings might work as an effective general deterrent, but (I'm going out on a limb here) it's simply not good public policy.

Making the use of mobile phones on public transportation a crime would certainly seem likely to accomplish the end of specific deterrence. Punishment for this conduct would seem likely to keep the person punished from committing that particular criminal act again. But that, of course, is not the end of the analysis.

As to incapacitation, incarceration as a justification for criminalizing the use of mobile phones would certainly work (inmates would not be riding public busses or subway cars), but it raises once again the question whether or not jail time is an appropriate sanction for such conduct as a matter of public policy.

Rehabilitation as a justification for such a criminal statute raises an interesting question. Can we "cure" people from using mobile phones in public? Wholly aside from the question whether or not we want to do that, is this the kind of conduct that is a proper subject for training and reeducation? Likely not.

With respect to retribution, just how antisocial is this behavior anyway? Arguably, since overly loud or obnoxious people on mobile phones are simply annoying rather than dangerous (as they would be if they were driving cars while talking on a mobile phone), the notions of just deserts and vengeance would not seem to justify criminal punishment in this particular setting.

Finally, of all the justifications for punishment, the expression of community values may come the closest to supporting this proposed criminal statute. But does your boss, the legislator, really believe that this sort of conduct demands criminal punishment in order to educate people about how wrong this conduct is? Do you? Maybe your employer does believe this. If so, maybe public policy would be best served if she loses her next reelection bid!

■ PROBLEM 1.2 ■

Twenty-two-year-old Joan Smith has been convicted of armed robbery. She held up an elderly woman at knife point and took her purse, which contained $42 and some change. She was arrested almost immediately, three blocks away. This is Smith's first arrest. A mother of two small children, she recently separated from her husband and is unemployed, having recently lost her part-time sales job. A pre-sentence report indicates that she uses narcotics occasionally and that she committed the robbery in order to get some money both for drugs and for food for her kids.

You are a law clerk to the sentencing judge who has the discretion to sentence Smith to anything from probation to 5 years in prison. Considering the justifications for punishment, what will you advise the judge?

Analysis

It is important to recognize at the outset that the justifications for punishment discussed thus far are not like mathematical formulae which, when properly used, will automatically produce a certain and defined end result. Rather, in this setting, they are simply useful guides for channeling the exercise of judicial discretion. They, hopefully, help judges (and lawyers who are arguing to judges) make fair and rational sentencing decisions, and avoid arbitrariness in sentences. It is, accordingly, neither certain nor even likely that any two judges using these same justifications in identical factual situations would sentence exactly the same way. But use of these justifications would nonetheless help educate and focus the analysis of both of these judges in desirable ways.

Considering general deterrence, the basic question is what sort of sentence would serve best to deter others (not Joan Smith herself) from engaging in criminal behavior like this? One could argue that people who are narcotics addicts and/or who are committing criminal acts to feed their hungry children can't be easily deterred from such actions. But that sort of argument applies the general deterrence theory too narrowly. A severe sentence for armed robbery might well serve to deter some non-addicted, non-parents-of-hungry-children from engaging in such conduct.

Of course, as with the analysis in Problem 1.1, even if a strict criminal penalty might conceivably have a general deterrent effect, that does not mean necessarily that it is appropriate. Judges need to weigh the nature of the particular crime and of the offender herself against the social value presumably gained in (maybe) deterring others in setting a sentence. The crime here is a serious one: armed robbery. The victim could have been seriously hurt or even killed. And the victim was elderly and likely defenseless. But, the offender's circumstances are sad and troubling, too: her drug use, her unemployment, her starving children.

Moreover, the notion of specific deterrence might well dictate a heavier rather than a lighter sentence here. The sentencing judge has to make a judgment about what sort of punishment would most effectively (and fairly) ensure that Joan Smith (not others) would not rob again. And, of course, as to incapacitation, a sentence including incarceration would certainly keep Joan Smith off the streets for whatever period of time she was behind bars.

Rehabilitation? Would it work here? Did Joan Smith's problem stem from a "bad mind." Or might it have been due instead to her drug use and/or her desperation and the need to feed her children? What are the odds that Smith could be "trained"—in a prison setting—to stop abusing drugs, at least? Based on our experience, they may not be high. Indeed, maybe more to the point, would a long stretch in prison really "cure" her . . . or might it instead make her life and her prospects and her odds of recidivism upon release worse?

With respect to retribution, there is no question but that Joan Smith committed a heinous crime. She robbed an elderly woman, threatening her with a knife. Certainly the concepts of just deserts and vengeance would justify serious criminal punishment in this setting.

Finally, the expression of community values justification for criminal punishment cuts two ways. Certainly we want to reaffirm our strong abhorrence of the use of this sort of antisocial behavior. On the other hand, we might also want to demonstrate our empathy (if not our forgiveness) given the circumstance that may have caused Smith to act by moderating the severity of her sentence. That is an educative lesson, too, of course.

How does this conclude then? Well, it depends on the judge. One might very well anticipate, on balance, that the nature of the crime (knife point, elderly victim) which supports sending a deterrent message will be balanced against the circumstances of the offense (the defendant's addiction, her and our concern about the children) which make prospects for rehabilitation highly speculative in coming up with an appropriate sentence. How would you sentence someone like Joan Smith? It may be hard to believe right now, but someday, you may have to answer just that question.

POINTS TO REMEMBER

- Criminal law is largely statutory today, and often found in a Crimes Code.
- Felonies are more serious crimes than misdemeanors.
- Many MPC provisions have been adopted in Crimes Codes and are referenced in court decisions.
- The prosecution must prove every element of a crime beyond a reasonable doubt.
- Criminal law is different from civil law due primarily to stigma of criminal conviction and possibility of incarceration.
- Justifications for criminal punishment are: general deterrence; specific deterrence; incapacitation; rehabilitation; retribution; and expression of community values.
- Supreme Court has held death penalty constitutional on basis of retribution and general deterrence and concluded that it is not "cruel and unusual," but some states don't use it.

CHAPTER 2

Actus Reus

To establish that a crime has been committed, the prosecution must prove beyond a reasonable doubt that the accused committed a criminal act or failed to perform an act he or she was legally required to perform. It is not enough that the accused simply thought about committing a crime or wanted to commit a crime.

This criminal act has traditionally been called the "actus reus" element of the crime. The actus reus is usually established by statute. Sometimes there is more than one actus reus for a single criminal offense.

A. VOLUNTARY ACT

The actus reus of a crime must be committed voluntarily. Or to put it another way, if the accused shows that his or her actions were "involuntary," no crime has been made out. In most jurisdictions, the prosecution has the burden of proving that the accused acted voluntarily. However, in a minority of jurisdictions, involuntariness is instead an affirmative defense, i.e. it must be raised and proved by the accused rather than by the prosecution.

When is an act involuntary? An act is voluntary if it is a product of a person's free will, manifested by a corresponding, external body movement. Conversely, an act is involuntary if it is *not* a product of a person's free will, manifested by a corresponding, external body movement.

The Model Penal Code (MPC) lists the following as a partial list of involuntary acts: "(a) a reflex or convulsion; (b) a bodily movement during unconsciousness or sleep; (c) conduct during hypnosis or resulting from hypnotic suggestion; (d) a bodily movement that otherwise is not a product of the effort or determination of the actor, either conscious or habitual." MPC § 2.01(2).

If an accused person can prove that he or she killed someone while sleepwalking or otherwise in an unconscious state, for example (no easy task!), such a killing act would be involuntary, and no crime has been committed.

Relationship to mens rea. The involuntariness defense exists whether or not the accused had the intention to commit a crime. In fact, this defense exists even where the criminal offense in question is a strict liability offense and does not require proof of any criminal intent (mens rea) at all. *See* Chapter 3 (Mens Rea). Involuntariness negates the actus reus of a crime, not the mens rea.

B. POSSESSION

Many criminal statutes contain an actus reus that revolves around possession of something, e.g. possession of narcotics, or possession of firearms by a convicted felon.

When is the act of possession made out? To establish a possessory act, the prosecution must establish that the accused was aware of his or her possession of a contraband item to a degree sufficient to be able to exercise control over it, and that he or she acted knowingly and voluntarily in possessing it. MPC § 2.01(4) provides that "[p]ossession is an act . . . if the possessor knowingly procured or received the thing possessed or was aware of his control thereof for a sufficient period to have been able to terminate his possession."

Joint possession. Contraband can be possessed by more than one person simultaneously when it is found in a place where more than one person is shown to have been aware of its existence and to have exercised control over it.

Constructive possession. A person can be guilty of possession of contraband even when it is not found on his or her person or immediate vicinity. Contraband is possessed constructively when it is found in a place where the accused is shown to have been aware of its existence and to have exercised control over it.

Contraband can be possessed jointly and constructively at the same time.

C. STATUS-BASED CRIMES

The Supreme Court has ruled that an accused person cannot be convicted of being addicted to narcotics, since addiction is a "status" not an "act." *Robinson v. California,* 370 U.S. 660 (1962). Such a status could be the result of disease, or contracted innocently or involuntarily. An addicted baby might be born to a narcotics-using mother, for example, and be addicted through no fault of his or her own.

An accused person can be convicted, however, for an act that is related to his or her status, e.g. for public drunkenness, even though that act was a result of the accused's status of chronic alcoholism. *Powell v. Texas*, 392 U.S. 514 (1968).

D. OMISSIONS

Where an accused person has failed to act, he or she has not committed a criminal act and ordinarily cannot be convicted of a crime based upon that failure. This is a so-called "omission." *Twitter, Inc. v. Taamneh*, 143 S.Ct. 1206, 1221 (2023) ("Our legal system generally does not impose liability for mere omissions, inactions, or nonfeasance; the law does not impose a generalized duty to rescue").

There is an exception to this general rule, however, where the accused person has failed to perform an act that he or she was legally required to perform. *Twitter, Inc. v. Taamneh*, 143 S.Ct. 1206, 1221 (2023) ("inaction can be culpable in the face of some independent duty to act").

Omissions generally. Criminal statutes do not usually require people to help other people, even other people who are in trouble. For example, even if a person has ample means to help someone who is homeless or who has been in a car accident, he or she has no obligation that is enforceable at criminal law to come to that person's assistance. Similarly, someone who can swim (but does not have a duty to act, like a lifeguard) is not responsible at criminal law for his or her failure to come to the aid of a drowning swimmer.

Exceptions: duty-to-aid statutes. A few states and municipalities have, however, legislated limited exceptions to the general rule, requiring people who can act without harm to themselves to help victims who are being harmed.

Exceptions: legal duties. A person does have a duty to act—and, hence, can be convicted for a failure to act—in the following circumstances:

- where a statute imposes such a duty, e.g. the obligation of a doctor to report to the police patients with gunshot wounds;
- where a close "status relationship" exists, e.g. parent-child;
- where a contractual obligation exists, e.g. the contractual duty of a lifeguard to come to the aid of drowning swimmers;

- where a person takes the initiative and performs an act, e.g. by coming to the aid of a person in distress (sometimes called "assumption of duty");
- and where the actor has created the peril that confronts the victim, e.g. by running him over.

Limitations on the duty to act. A person cannot be convicted for failing to act, however, even though he or she has a duty to act, where he or she is unaware of the need to act, or does not have the physical capacity to do whatever is necessary to provide such aid.

Someone who cannot swim, for example, has not committed a crime when he or she does not try to jump in a pool and rescue a drowning swimmer. This is true even if the drowning swimmer is the person's child and, hence, a legal duty to act exists based upon that status relationship. A person is not required by the criminal law to take steps of which the person is not physically capable. However, that same person—watching his or her drowning child—might have committed a crime by failing to do something that he or she was physically capable of doing, e.g. calling for help.

Constitutional issues. The Supreme Court ruled in 1957 that a person cannot be convicted constitutionally for a failure to act where he or she had no reason to be aware that what he or she was doing was a violation of a criminal statute creating a legal duty to act, in that case, to register her presence as a "convicted person" in the city of Los Angeles. *Lambert v. California*, 355 U.S. 225 (1957).

The *Lambert* decision does *not* mean that people are not responsible for failing to follow criminal laws of which they are unaware. That is *not* the law. *See* Chapter 4 (Mistake). Rather, the limited *Lambert* holding applies only to excuse failures to act in the rare cases where a person is not reasonably on notice that a criminal or regulatory statute may exist to govern his or her conduct.

ACTUS REUS CHECKLIST

A. **The Basics**—all criminal offenses contain one or more act requirements.

1. **Actus Reus**—traditional name for act requirement.
2. **Thought Crimes**—do not exist; there must be actus reus.
3. **Statutes**—actus reus is usually set out in criminal statute.

B. **Voluntary Act**—actus reus of criminal offense must be committed voluntarily.

1. **Involuntary Act Defense**—if accused acted involuntarily, actus reus element is not established and no crime.

2. **Involuntariness Definition**—act is involuntary if it is *not* a product of person's free will, manifested by corresponding, external body movement.

3. **Examples**—sleepwalking, actions while unconscious, reflexes.

4. **Mens Rea Irrelevant**—involuntariness is defense whether or not accused possessed mens rea and whether or not crime is strict liability.

C. **Possession**—some crimes have actus reus requiring proof of possession of something.

1. **Possession Defined**—awareness of possession to degree sufficient to be able to exercise control, while acting knowingly and voluntarily.

2. **Joint Possession**—possession by more than one person simultaneously when item found in place where more than one person was aware of existence and exercised control over it.

3. **Constructive Possession**—possession of contraband when found not on or around accused, but in place where person was aware of existence and exercised control over it.

D. **Status-Based Crimes**—person cannot be convicted merely for "status," e.g. as a narcotics addict.

1. **Rationale**—status may be acquired as result of disease, or otherwise innocently or involuntarily without fault on part of accused.

2. **Status vs. Act**—person can be convicted for committing criminal offense based upon act that was result of status, e.g. public drunkenness.

E. **Omissions**—accused cannot ordinarily be convicted of crime based upon failure to act.

1. **Exceptions: Duty-to-Aid**—minority jurisdictions require people to assist victims being harmed.

2. **Exceptions: Legal Duties**—person can be convicted for failure to act where legal duty to act. Common legal duties:

   a. **Statute**—where statute imposes duty.

b. **Status**—where close "status relationship" exists.

c. **Contract**—where contractual obligation exists.

d. **Assumption of Duty**—where person takes initiative and performs act.

e. **Creation of Peril**—where actor has created peril that confronts victim.

3. **Limitations on Legal Duties**—inapplicable where person is unaware of need to act, or does not have physical capacity to help.

4. ***Lambert***—very limited defense excusing failures to act where legal duty when person not reasonably on notice that statute exists requiring action.

ILLUSTRATIVE PROBLEMS

These problems illustrate how the checklist points help to resolve questions involving the actus reus of a crime.

■ PROBLEM 2.1 ■

Serena Studds is a passenger in a car driven by her friend, Juanita Wilson. Over Studds' objections, Wilson drives the car and parks it in a garage which they both know is located on private property, and which has a sign posted on the front of it saying "No Trespassing." Both Studds and Wilson are arrested and prosecuted for the crime of trespass. Is Studds guilty of trespass?

Analysis

No.

Wholly aside from any other defense she might have (e.g., she may not have the mens rea for the crime of trespass, *see* Chapter 3 (Mens Rea)), Studds is not guilty of trespass because she was transported onto the property involuntarily. Her presence on the private property was not the product of her own free will, but rather was caused by Wilson's act of driving her onto the property over her objections.

■ PROBLEM 2.2 ■

Police officers, executing a lawful search warrant for narcotics, discover marijuana in a shoe box in Kevin Klein's bedroom closet. The bedroom is part of a two-bedroom apartment he shares with a roommate, Ashley Trubo. Are Klein and Trubo both guilty of possession of marijuana?

Analysis

If this is a jurisdiction where possession of marijuana is still criminalized, Klein is likely guilty of this crime. Assuming that a judge or jury believes that he knew that the marijuana was located in his closet (Kevin: "How did that get there?"), it was clearly situated in a place where he was able to exercise control over it. Hence, Klein was guilty of possession. That is true, moreover, even if it is established that the marijuana actually belonged to someone else, and it had simply been hidden—with his knowledge—in his bedroom closet.

Trubo may or may not be guilty of possession of marijuana, depending on the existence or absence of other circumstances. The fact that Klein possessed the marijuana and that it was located in Klein's bedroom does not necessarily clear Trubo of criminal responsibility. A person can be convicted of joint and constructive possession of contraband, even where it is not on her person or located in her immediate vicinity. What sort of access did she have to Klein's bedroom and to his closet? What evidence exists that she knew about the presence of the marijuana and, perhaps, that she might have used some of it or shared it with him or others? As this additional evidence cumulates, it might be possible to convict Trubo (as well as Klein) of the possession of the marijuana.

If, however, the prosecution can establish no other link on Trubo's part to the marijuana other than the fact that it was found in her roommate's separate bedroom, she is not likely to be found guilty of possession of marijuana.

■ PROBLEM 2.3 ■

Jean Stone and Elena Horensky observe a young person they do not know being assaulted by two men in a public park and they do nothing about it. They continue strolling through the park. Have Stone and Horensky committed a criminal act?

Analysis

No.

They have not acted. Rather, they have failed to act, a classic omission. Although what they did may be morally heinous, it is not punished by the criminal law in the absence of a specific duty-to-aid statute (only enacted in a minority of jurisdictions) or some other legal duty to act. As they did not know the victim and had no prior relationship with him or her, there is no evidence that there was any duty requiring them to act.

■ PROBLEM 2.4 ■

Amy Kelley's 82-year-old, profoundly disabled father is living with her in her home. She does not provide him with enough food and water to survive, and she does not help him to obtain the medications he needs to survive given his medical ailments. He cannot obtain these medications on his own, and he is unable to communicate with someone else to obtain them for him. He dies as a result.

Is Kelley responsible at criminal law for his death? Is she guilty of some form of homicide, for example?

Analysis

Probably not, but possibly yes.

There is no killing act present, the actus reus of homicide. *See* Chapter 12 (Homicide).

Here, Kelley did not do something to her father; rather, she failed to do something. She failed to give him sufficient food and hydration and medication to live. But, as in the preceding problem, this is an omission, a failure to act, and omissions are not ordinarily held to be culpable at criminal law. Unless, however, some exception to the general rule exists.

In some jurisdictions, for example, the relationship of adult child to parent has been deemed to be a cognizable status relationship. In jurisdictions like those, Kelley would indeed have a legal duty to act, and her failure to live up to that duty could be punished criminally, assuming that the other elements of a criminal offense are made out (e.g., mens rea and causation for homicide).

Similarly, if additional facts are present that are not set out in the problem itself, other legal duties might exist that could result in Kelley's failure to act being treated as a culpable actus reus. For example, perhaps Kelley has previously assumed the duty of caring for her father by feeding and medicating him, thus keeping other people (or institutions) from assuming that obligation. If that were deemed to be the case, a legal duty may be said to have existed.

Or, perhaps Kelley had some sort of contractual obligation to assist her father, e.g. maybe she was receiving money from a social services agency to care for him. In such an instance, her failure to act could then be viewed as a culpable actus reus because of the existence of that duty to act and, assuming once again the existence of the other elements of a criminal offense, she would be guilty of a crime. Involuntary manslaughter, perhaps. *See* Chapter 12 (Homicide).

POINTS TO REMEMBER

- A person's involuntary act does not establish the actus reus of a crime.
- Involuntariness is an actus reus defense, not a mens rea defense.
- An involuntariness defense can be made out whether or not accused had mens rea and whether or not crime is strict liability.
- Proof of possession of contraband requires awareness to a degree sufficient to be able to exercise control, while acting knowingly and voluntarily.
- A person can be convicted of possession jointly and/or constructively even if thing possessed is not on his or her person or nearby.
- A person cannot be convicted of crime based merely upon status, but can be convicted for criminal act resulting from that status.
- A person cannot ordinarily be convicted of crime based upon an omission.
- A person's failure to act can be criminal where: legal duty to act; awareness of need to act; and physically capable of acting.

CHAPTER 3

Mens Rea

To establish that a crime has been committed, the prosecutor ordinarily must prove beyond a reasonable doubt that the accused acted with a particular "mens rea" (or culpable mental state, sometimes also termed "scienter"), as required by law. *See Ruan v. U.S.*, 142 S. Ct. 2370, 2377 (2022) (" '[S]cienter,' means the degree of knowledge necessary to make a person criminally responsible for his or her acts.").

The traditional view has long been that a person should not be found guilty of a serious criminal offense unless he or she possessed such a blameworthy mens rea. *See, e.g., Ruan v. U.S.*, 142 S. Ct. 2370, 2376–77 (2022) ("[A]s a general matter, our criminal law seeks to punish the 'vicious will.' With few exceptions, 'wrongdoing must be conscious to be criminal.' Indeed, we have said that consciousness of wrongdoing is a principle 'as universal and persistent in mature systems of [criminal] law as belief in freedom of the human will and a consequent ability and duty of the normal individual to choose between good and evil.' "); *Rehaif v. U.S.*, 139 S. Ct. 2191, 2196 (2019). Indeed, the more blameworthy the mens rea, typically, the more serious the crime that the accused person has committed.

A. THE EVOLUTION OF MENS REA CONCEPTS

At early common law, the concept of mens rea indicated simply the existence of a guilty mind or generalized wickedness. But it did not take long for courts to decide that such a non-specific showing was insufficient for conviction.

Courts began to require—as they do today—proof of a specific mens rea (not simply general wickedness) in order to support conviction for a serious crime. In the well-known nineteenth-century decision in *Regina v. Faulkner*, 13 Cox Crim. Cas. 550 (1877), for example, a majority of the appellate judges sitting on the case concluded that a sailor who burned up a ship through his careless use of an open flame while stealing rum from a cask could not be convicted for burning the ship without a specific showing that he satisfied the specific mens rea required for that crime as set out in the underlying criminal statute. The fact that Faulkner was clearly a bad man engaged in a theft when he caused the fire was not a sufficient showing of mens rea to support his conviction.

Model Penal Code mens rea approach. Before the Model Penal Code (MPC) was enacted, most states used many, many different and often overly-nuanced terms of art to describe the necessary mens rea required to establish a crime, e.g. "maliciously," "feloniously," "unlawfully," "fraudulently," "wantonly," and "willfully." Some still do. But what is the difference between a willful and a wanton act? It was not easy to say.

As a result, the drafters of the MPC urged jurisdictions to standardize mens rea terms, distinguishing only four levels of mens rea culpability: purpose; knowledge; recklessness; and negligence. MPC § 2.02(1). Many states followed this general MPC lead and (tried to) standardize the mens rea element in many of the crimes in their Crimes Codes in this regard.

Purpose. MPC § 2.02(1)(a) provides that "(i) if the element involves the nature of his conduct or a result thereof, it is his conscious object to engage in conduct of that nature or to cause such a result; and (ii) if the element involves the attendant circumstances, he is aware of the existence of such circumstances or he believes or hopes that they exist."

Purpose is the most difficult mens rea term to satisfy under the MPC. It is referred to as "intentional" conduct in some jurisdictions, e.g. to convict an accused of first-degree murder in most jurisdictions, the prosecution must prove the accused person's actual intention to kill his victim. An accidental, unintentional, reckless, or negligent killing will not suffice. *See* Chapter 12 (Homicide).

Knowledge. MPC § 2.02(1)(b) provides that "(i) if the element involves the nature of his conduct or the attendant circumstances, he is aware that his conduct is of that nature or that such circumstances exist; and (ii) if the element involves a result of his conduct, he is aware that it is practically certain that his conduct will cause such a result."

Significantly, unlike acting purposefully, proving that an accused knowingly acted or caused a particular result does not require the prosecution to establish that the act or result was the actor's "conscious object."

Recklessness. MPC § 2.02(1)(c) provides that "[a] person acts recklessly with respect to a material element of an offense when he consciously disregards a substantial and unjustifiable risk that the material element exists or will result from his conduct. The risk must be of such a nature and degree that, considering the nature and purpose of the actor's conduct and the circumstances known to him, its disregard involves a gross deviation from the standard of conduct that a law-abiding person would observe in the actor's situation."

In many jurisdictions, the element of malice required to establish the commission of a murder, *see* Chapter 12 (Homicide), can be implied from an accused person's killing act committed with gross recklessness.

Negligence. MPC § 2.02(1)(d) provides that "[a] person acts negligently with respect to a material element of an offense when he should be aware of a substantial and unjustifiable risk that the material element exists or will result from his conduct. The risk must be of such a nature and degree that the actor's failure to perceive it, considering the nature and purpose of his conduct and the circumstances known to him, involves a gross deviation from the standard of care that a reasonable person would observe in the actor's situation."

Recklessness vs. negligence. It is important to be able to distinguish between recklessness and negligence in the criminal law. Most significantly, the concept of recklessness contains a subjective element, i.e. the accused must have "*consciously*" disregarded a "substantial and unjustifiable" risk in order to have acted recklessly. Negligence in the criminal law, on the other hand, is strictly an objective concept, i.e. to be negligent, the accused *should have* been aware of a "substantial and unjustifiable risk," rather than having actually been aware of the risk in order to "consciously" disregard it, as is required to establish recklessness.

Criminal vs. civil. You should also distinguish between the concepts of civil negligence (sometimes called "ordinary negligence") and criminal negligence (sometimes called "gross negligence"). Criminal negligence (and criminal recklessness) require proof of a "gross" disregard of reasonable behavior; tort law does not.

Concurrence of act and intent. The actus reus, *see* Chapter 2 (Actus Reus), and the mens rea elements of a criminal offense must concur in order to create culpability. The fact that an accused had a culpable intent at one time but did not take a culpable action until some time later when the actor no longer had that intent, for example, does not establish the commission of a crime. The bad act and the bad intent must occur at the same time.

What other elements does the mens rea element modify? A mens rea element in a criminal statute modifies each of the other elements of the crime unless there is evidence of a clear contrary legislative intent. *See Flores-Figueroa v. U.S.*, 556 U.S. 646, 650

(2009) ("In ordinary English, where a transitive verb has an object, listeners in most contexts assume that an adverb (such as knowingly) that modifies the transitive verb tells the listener how the subject performed the entire action, including the object as set forth in the sentence.").

For example, if a statute criminalizes "knowingly creating a public nuisance in a public place," in the absence of a court finding a contrary legislative intent, the prosecution would have to establish that the accused knew that he or she was creating a public nuisance *and* knew that he or she was in a public place when creating that nuisance. *See, e.g., Ruan v. U.S.*, 142 S. Ct. 2370, 2377 (2022) ("We have held that a word such as 'knowingly' modifies not only the words directly following it, but also those other statutory terms that separate wrongful from innocent acts.").

B. STRICT LIABILITY

Some criminal offenses—a minority—do not require proof of any mens rea at all. These are strict liability offenses.

Because we normally associate blameworthiness with the existence of some level of criminal intent, most crimes do require proof of a mens rea, particularly most serious criminal offenses. However, at least one very serious criminal offense, statutory rape, is usually a strict liability offense. *See* Chapter 11 (Sex Crimes).

Common law crimes. The Supreme Court has ruled that crimes with common law origins, e.g. larceny, should be interpreted by courts as requiring proof of the same mens rea that they had at common law, in the absence of a contrary legislative intent. *See Morissette v. U.S.*, 342 U.S. 246 (1952). Even if the statute does not expressly contain a mens rea element, the presumption is that the legislature intended to incorporate the common law mens rea. *See, e.g., Ruan v. U.S.*, 142 S. Ct. 2370, 2377 (2022); *Rehaif v. U.S.*, 139 S. Ct. 2191, 2195 (2019) ("[W]e start from a longstanding presumption, traceable to the common law, that Congress intends to require a defendant to possess a culpable mental state regarding 'each of the statutory elements that criminalize otherwise innocent conduct.' ").

Public welfare or regulatory offenses. Legislatures often enact strict liability criminal offenses in areas relating to the public welfare, particularly the regulation of potentially harmful or injurious items. The notion is that people who are involved in these areas, e.g. the manufacture of goods, should be on notice of the likelihood that such regulation exists.

Whether or not to include a mens rea element in a criminal offense is a legislative judgment. All the courts are supposed to do in this regard is to determine legislative intention.

Where a criminal statute does not contain a mens rea element in its text, but it is found that people would likely be on notice of such regulation, courts construe that statute as strict liability. *See, e.g., U.S. v. Freed,* 401 U.S. 601 (1971) (possession of hand grenades). But where such a criminal statute exists, and it is deemed unlikely that people would be on notice of the likelihood of regulation, courts construe those statutes *not* to be strict liability. *See, e.g., Staples v. U.S.,* 511 U.S. 600 (1994) (possession of automatic weapons).

C. INTOXICATION & DRUGGED CONDITION

In a majority of jurisdictions, the fact that an accused was intoxicated or drugged at the time he or she committed the criminal act in question is deemed to be a defense—negativing the mens rea element—if the crime was a specific intent crime, but not a defense if the crime was a general intent (or strict liability) crime.

In some jurisdictions, however, intoxication or drugged condition is never a defense to any crime.

General vs. specific intent crimes. The distinction between general and specific intent crimes is often a fine one, and varies by jurisdiction. Typically, a crime is deemed to be general intent when the mens rea requires only the intent to do the act that causes the harm, e.g. punching someone as an assault. In contrast, a crime is deemed to be specific intent when the required mens rea requires proof of some additional intent beyond committing the act that causes the harm, e.g. assault with intent to rape.

Degree of intoxication. In jurisdictions recognizing an intoxication or drugged condition defense, the fact that someone had been drinking or using drugs at the time of the crime is not sufficient, in and of itself, to make out the defense. An accused must establish that he or she was so deeply intoxicated or drugged that he or she did not possess the mens rea necessary to establish the charged offenses.

MENS REA CHECKLIST

A. **The Basics**—showing of general wickedness not enough to establish mens rea.

1. **Mens Rea**—traditional name for mental state requirement ("scienter").

2. **Sufficient Showing**—prosecution must prove specific mens rea element beyond a reasonable doubt.

3. **MPC Tests**—four levels of intentionality to be used as mens rea tests: purpose; knowledge; recklessness; and negligence.

    a. **Purpose**—accused's "conscious object" was to commit criminal act charged.

    b. **Knowledge**—accused was aware that nature of conduct was like that charged or was "practically certain" that it would cause criminal result.

    c. **Recklessness**—accused "consciously" disregarded substantial and unjustifiable risk of committing or causing criminal act which was "gross deviation" from what reasonable person would do.

    d. **Negligence**—accused "should" have been aware of substantial and unjustifiable risk of committing or causing criminal act which was "gross deviation" from what reasonable person would do.

    e. **Recklessness vs. Negligence**—for recklessness, accused has to actually be aware of risk of criminal conduct (subjective test), while for negligence, accused merely should have been aware (objective test).

4. **Concurrence of Act & Intent**—mens rea and actus reus must exist at same time to establish commission of crime.

5. **Modification of Elements**—mens rea element modifies other elements unless contrary legislative intent.

B. **Strict Liability**—most criminal offenses have mens rea element, but some do not.

1. **Common Law Origins**—if crime taken from common law contains no mens rea element, mens rea is still presumed to exist unless legislature states otherwise.

2. **Public Welfare Offenses**—if regulatory offense contains no mens rea element, it is strict liability if people are on notice that regulations of this sort exist, but not strict liability otherwise.

3. **Legislative Intention Controls**—legislature decides whether crime is strict liability or not; courts only interpret legislative intent.

C. **Intoxication & Drugged Condition**—mens rea defense in most jurisdictions if crime was specific intent, but not if general intent (or strict liability).

1. **General vs. Specific Intent**—general when conviction requires only proof of intent to commit act that causes the harm; specific when proof is required of an additional intent beyond committing act that causes the harm.

2. **Sufficiency**—intoxication or drugged condition must be so extreme that accused did not possess prescribed mens rea.

ILLUSTRATIVE PROBLEMS

The following problems illustrate how the checklist points help to resolve questions relating to the mens rea of a crime.

■ PROBLEM 3.1 ■

Eldon Jeffries has been charged with first-degree murder in the death of Karen Hite, a six year-old child. In this jurisdiction, first-degree murder requires proof of the mens rea element of purposeful conduct, as defined by the MPC. What happened was that Jeffries had been drinking heavily at a bar for five hours. He then staggered to his car, got in and drove off wildly and erratically, ultimately speeding right through a red light at sixty m.p.h. and smashing into another car, killing Hite.

Is Jeffries guilty of first degree murder?

Analysis

No.

The actus reus of homicide is a killing act resulting in the death of a human being. *See* Chapter 12 (Homicide). To commit this act purposefully, Jeffries would have had to have (under the MPC) the "conscious object to . . . cause such a result." Begging the question for a moment of how "conscious" he actually was due to his heavy drinking, it is clear from these facts that it was not his conscious object to crash into the victim's car and kill her. Accordingly, he is not guilty of first-degree murder. Of course, he could well be guilty of a different homicide crime, involuntary manslaughter perhaps, with a mens rea of recklessness.

Then there's the question of the relevance of Jeffries' probable intoxication. Of course, he doesn't need an intoxication defense to negative mens rea, as it is already clear that he has not acted purposefully in any event, as discussed above. But let's change the facts a little bit. Suppose that—in his drunken state—he saw little

Karen in her car seat in the car and plowed right into her, intending to kill her for some irrational reason. Hence, his conduct was purposeful, unlike the initial facts. Could he defend on the basis of intoxication? The answer is "yes" . . . but, assuming two things.

First, does this jurisdiction accept intoxication as a defense? If it doesn't, then of course, he has no defense. But let's assume that it does. If it does, then, second, was he sufficiently intoxicated, not just tipsy, but so inebriated that he really couldn't possess the appropriate mens rea for this crime? Let's assume once again that he was. Let's assume that he just polished off a fifth of gin, four beers, and two cosmopolitans with tiny pink umbrellas in them and pretty much no longer knew what planet he inhabited.

Well, then we're left with the final question: is first degree murder a specific intent crime? If so (and assuming, again, positive answers to the two additional points addressed in the prior paragraph), then Jeffries does have a good intoxication defense to first degree murder. And, in fact, first degree murder *is* considered a specific intent crime because the actor's intention goes beyond the assaultive conduct being committed and includes the further intention that that conduct result in the victim's death.

Finally and once again, please note that the fact that Jeffries may not be guilty of first degree murder due to his intoxication, does not absolve him necessarily of his potential culpability for other homicide offenses which are not specific intent crimes.

■ PROBLEM 3.2 ■

Demont Wood was driving his motor scooter to school when his front tire hit a rut in the road and blew out. The scooter then careened into a crosswalk and struck and injured two pedestrians.

Was Wood culpable criminally for acting recklessly? Negligently?

Analysis

Wood was not reckless. To have acted recklessly, Wood would have had to have been consciously aware (subjective focus) of the risk that this injurious result would occur. There is no evidence in this problem that that was the case. The result changes, of course, if Wood had been aware that the rut was there in the road and might cause this sort of problem, but tried to drive through it anyway, despite the risk.

Negligence? *Should* Wood have known of this risk (objective focus)? There is not enough evidence on these facts to find criminal negligence either. What additional facts might help to establish gross negligence? Well, what if he should have realized that his front tire was bald and might blow out at any time? Something like that would probably do it.

■ PROBLEM 3.3 ■

Xylon Corporation has been charged with a state environmental crime by the state water pollution control agency for allowing organic phosphorus compounds to be discharged into a local stream in an amount exceeding statutory limits. Xylon concedes the excessive discharge, but explains that the machinery that ordinarily prevented such pollution was malfunctioning for two days and they did not discover the problem until the end of the second day, when they immediately repaired it. The state agency has confirmed that this explanation is accurate.

Is this a good defense to a criminal charge?

Analysis

Probably not.

Most regulatory criminal offenses like this one are strict liability offenses. It is perfectly lawful for legislatures to enact criminal statutes that do not contain mens rea elements. If, indeed, this statute is strict liability, it doesn't matter why Xylon broke the law, i.e. whether or not it had a blameworthy intent. It only matters that the corporation did in fact violate the law, as it readily concedes that it did.

Of course, legislatures are also free to include a mens rea in a regulatory statute if that is what they want to do. If this statue does in fact contain a mens rea provision, it is unlikely that the state agency could prove that Xylon was guilty of anything more than criminally negligent behavior, if that. To establish such criminal negligence, the agency would have to prove that Xylon should have known (an objective test again, *see* Problem 3.2) of the risk that this malfunction would occur and that an impermissible amount of effluents would be discharged into the stream.

We would need additional information to determine whether Xylon employees should have known this. Was there a warning system on the equipment? Did it register the problem? Was it checked regularly? Should it have been? These are the sorts of questions we might have to ask in order to determine whether criminal negligence existed.

POINTS TO REMEMBER

- Different levels of criminal intention (mens rea) exist and the prosecution must prove beyond a reasonable doubt the mens rea established for the crime charged.
- The MPC distinguishes between purpose, knowledge, recklessness and negligence.
- Recklessness requires that the accused was actually aware of the risk of his criminal conduct, while negligence requires only that the accused should have been aware of the risk.
- Mens rea and actus reus have to exist at the same time for a crime to exist.
- Mens rea elements modify the other statutory elements unless the legislature intended otherwise.
- Legislatures decide whether criminal offenses are strict liability, courts only interpret legislative intention.
- Former common law offenses with a mens rea requirement are presumed not to be strict liability.
- Public welfare offenses without an express mens rea are presumed to be strict liability unless people would not be on notice that such regulation exists.
- In most jurisdictions, intoxication or drugged condition is a defense for specific intent crimes, but not for general intent crimes.
- To make a good intoxication or drugged condition defense, the accused must have been so extremely intoxicated or drugged that it was impossible for the accused to possess the mental state required for commission of the crime.

CHAPTER 4

Mistake

When (but only when) a criminal offense includes a mens rea element, an accused person may defend successfully when being charged with that crime by creating a reasonable doubt about whether he or she possessed the required mental intent when the criminal act occurred. *See* Chapter 3 (Mens Rea).

One way to make this defense is to show that the accused did not think that he or she was acting with the requisite mens rea due to a mistaken belief about relevant factual circumstances. This is often called a mistake of fact defense.

In contrast, an accused person's mistaken belief about the applicable law that applies to his or her conduct—a mistake of law—is not a good mens rea defense to a criminal charge.

"In its legal usage, 'mistake' includes errors 'of law or fact,' " but "the difference between 'mistake of fact' and 'mistake of law' is well known and both lay and legal dictionaries identify them as distinct categories." *Kemp v. United States*, 142 S. Ct. 1856, 1862 (2022).

A. MISTAKE OF FACT

A mistake of fact defense is one way of trying to negative the mens rea element of a criminal offense. A criminal defendant might argue that he or she did not act intentionally (when intentional conduct is the required mens rea) because it was not his or her conscious desire to commit the criminal act or obtain the criminal result at issue. *See* Chapter 3 (Mens Rea). A defendant using a mistake of fact defense is arguing further that the required mens rea did not exist because he or she honestly believed—mistakenly—that circumstances existed that did not make the act criminal (or, at least, not the criminal offense that was actually charged).

For example, someone accused of first degree murder might argue that they lacked the intentionality necessary to establish that offense when shooting and killing a victim because he or she thought that the gun used was unloaded. They might argue, perhaps, that their intent was really only to scare the victim.

If the jury believes this story about mistaken belief, the required mens rea did not exist and the accused should not be found guilty of first degree murder. Of course, this defendant might well be guilty of a different crime, even another homicide crime that includes a different mens rea. Depending on the facts, second degree murder perhaps, with a recklessness mens rea, might have been committed. *See* Chapter 12 (Homicide). Or assault certainly. *See* Chapter 10 (Assault).

Reasonableness requirement. Notably, however, in some jurisdictions in some circumstances, an accused trying to make a mistake of fact defense must establish not only that he or she honestly believed in the mistaken circumstance that negatives the mens rea required for the offense charged (a subjective test), but he or she must also establish that such a mistaken belief was reasonable as well (an objective test).

Instructions to the jury. Trial judges often do *not* instruct juries on the elements of a mistake of fact defense where they believe that the jury will already be considering the mistake issue in deciding whether the elements of the crime have been made out. For example, if a jury has been instructed that the prosecution must prove that the accused "purposely" shot and killed a victim and the accused is defending by arguing that she didn't know the gun was loaded, the jury would not find that the accused acted purposefully if the jurors believed that the accused didn't know the gun was loaded. As a result, the judge might well decide that a *separate* mistake of fact defense instruction was unnecessary.

Common law. At common law, mistake of fact was deemed to be a defense to a specific intent crime, *see* Chapter 3 (Mens Rea), when the accused could establish simply that he or she honestly believed in a mistaken circumstance that negatived the mens rea required for the offense charged (a subjective approach).

However, mistake of fact was deemed to be a defense to a general intent crime, *see* Chapter 3 (Mens Rea), only when the accused could establish *both* that he or she honestly believed in a mistaken circumstance that negatived the mens rea required for the offense charged (a subjective approach) *and* that such a mistaken belief was reasonable as well (an objective approach).

Model Penal Code. Model Penal Code (MPC) § 2.04(1) provides that "[i]gnorance or mistake as to a matter of fact . . . is a defense if: (a) the ignorance or mistake negatives the purpose, knowledge, belief, recklessness or negligence required to establish a material element of the offense; or (b) the law provides that the state of mind established by such ignorance or mistake constitutes a defense."

Since both recklessness and negligence contain objective elements, an accused person seeking to defend against a charge requiring proof of one of those mens reas would have to, *inter alia*, satisfy an objective test, i.e. did the accused honestly *and reasonably* believe in the mistaken circumstances that absolve him or her of culpability?

In contrast, someone accused of a criminal offense with a mens rea of purposeful or knowing conduct under the MPC would only have to establish his or her honest (not necessarily reasonable) belief in the mistaken circumstances in order to make out a good defense.

Strict liability. There is no mistake of fact defense to strict liability offenses. Mistake of fact is a mens rea defense and strict liability crimes have no mens rea. (Strict liability is discussed in Chapter 3 (Mens Rea)).

Since statutory rape is a strict liability offense in most jurisdictions, *see* Chapter 11 (Sex Crimes), there ordinarily is no mistake of fact defense to that crime (e.g. "I thought she looked older than 16").

B. MISTAKE OF LAW

The general rule is that mistake of law is no defense to criminal conduct. If an accused person commits a criminal act believing that it is not criminal, that is simply no defense to a criminal charge.

Distinguishing mistake of fact. If a person possessed illegal narcotics believing—mistakenly—that it was lawful to do so, that is a mistake-of-law argument, and it is not a good defense. If a person possessed narcotics believing reasonably that it was a lawful substance to possess, that is a mistake-of-fact argument, and it is a good defense, assuming that the crime is not a strict liability offense. *See* discussion in 4(A), *supra*.

Reliance on official permission. In some jurisdictions, an accused is entitled to defend against criminal charges on the ground that he or she mistakenly relied on the advice of an appropriate public official. This is sometimes called an "estoppel defense."

Knowledge of law as an element. In rare cases, where a legislature has made actual knowledge that a person's conduct is unlawful an element of a crime, mistake of law is a defense but only because it expressly negatives that element.

MISTAKE CHECKLIST

A. **Mistake of Fact**—one way of negativing mens rea.

1. **Depends on Mens Rea**—honest belief in mistaken circumstances must negative the particular mens rea of offense.
2. **Common Law Approach**—defense to specific intent crime when honest belief in mistake negativing mens rea; defense to general intent crime when honest and reasonable belief.
3. **MPC Approach**—elements of mistake defense depend upon particular mens rea element; reasonable mistaken belief required for recklessness and negligence.
4. **Strict Liability**—no mistake of fact defense.
5. **Jury Instructions**—mistake of fact may be covered in instruction on elements of crime charged.

B. **Mistake of Law**—not a defense.

1. **Distinguish Mistake of Fact**—mistake of fact defense relies on honest but mistaken belief in circumstances negativing mens rea; mistake of law is mistaken belief in lawfulness of conduct.
2. **Official Permission**—sometimes fact that accused was told officially that conduct was not criminal offense is good defense.
3. **Knowledge as Element**—good defense where legislature has made knowledge of illegality element of the crime.

ILLUSTRATIVE PROBLEMS

The following problems illustrate how the checklist points help to resolve questions relating to mistake issues.

■ PROBLEM 4.1 ■

Yolanda Juarez was arrested for the act of criminal trespass in a public park when she was found walking her dog one night in a public park after its posted closing hours. Juarez argues that she knew that she wasn't allowed in the park after closing hours, but she didn't realize that she was actually in the park. She thought that the field where she was walking was not part of the park property. There weren't any obvious signs that indicated otherwise.

Is this a good defense?

Analysis

It depends.

First, if the criminal trespass in a public park statute is a strict liability offense, it doesn't matter that she didn't intend to commit this crime. It is a strict liability offense, and mistake of fact is no defense.

Second, if this statute contains a mens rea element, the key is determining what that mens rea is. If, for example, the statute prohibits intentional trespassory actions, then her mistaken belief would be a good defense, negativing the mens rea of the offense, assuming that the jury believes her story. But, if the statute punishes reckless or negligence trespassory conduct, her story that she had a mistaken belief that she was not in the park would not only have to be believed by the jury (a subjective test), but would have to be considered a reasonably mistaken belief as well (an objective test). *See* Chapter 3 (Mens Rea).

What would make such a mistaken belief reasonable? The absence of a fence or obvious park boundaries, for example. Or the fact that there were no posted signs perhaps. Or maybe that there were signs but they were obscured by vegetation. Or maybe the fact that many people in the vicinity walked their dogs at night in this area and it appeared to all that it was not part of the park. Circumstances of that nature would help to establish the reasonableness of such a mistaken belief and help Juarez to make a successful mistake of fact defense to this charge.

■ PROBLEM 4.2 ■

Although there was a sign on the roadway indicating that cars could not turn left at a particular intersection (No Left Turn), Seymour Schwartz made an illegal left turn at that intersection anyway late one evening, because he honestly believed that the traffic laws prohibiting making such otherwise illegal turns did not apply when it was past midnight and no other cars were anywhere in the vicinity.

The police officer who stopped Schwartz and issued him a criminal traffic citation told him that that was not the law and that he faced a $250 fine for making an improper left turn.

Assuming that Schwartz's mistaken belief that he could make such a turn was reasonable, does he have a good defense to this charge?

Analysis

No.

Mistake of law is no defense.

■ PROBLEM 4.3 ■

Although there was a sign on the roadway indicating that cars could not turn left at a particular intersection (No Left Turn—7 am to 7 pm), Sandra Schwartz made an illegal left turn at that intersection anyway early one evening, because she honestly believed—mistakenly—that it was after 7 pm.

The police officer who stopped Schwartz and issued her a criminal traffic citation told her that her mistaken belief in the time was totally irrelevant and that she faced a $250 fine for making an improper left turn.

Assuming that Schwartz's mistaken belief that it was after 7 pm was reasonable, e.g. her dashboard clock said 7:02 but the police officer's watch showed 6:58, does she have a good defense to this charge?

Analysis

Yes, depending however upon the terms of the underlying criminal statute. This slight change in the facts from Problem 4.2 makes this a mistake of fact case rather than a mistake of law case.

A mistake of fact defense relies on an honest but mistaken belief in circumstances negativing mens rea. Assuming that the underlying criminal statute in question is not strict liability (which it may be), Schwartz's honest and reasonable mistaken belief in what the time actually was would be a good mistake of fact defense.

Mistake of law, in contrast, is a mistaken belief in what the law is. Schwartz knew full well what the law was. That wasn't the issue. She was simply mistaken about a fact: the correct time.

POINTS TO REMEMBER

- Mistake of fact can be good defense; mistake of law is not good defense.
- Mistake of fact does not apply to strict liability offenses.

- Judge may not instruct on mistake of fact where the issue is already covered in the instruction on the crime charged.
- Mistake of fact must be reasonable where mens rea focus upon unreasonable behavior, e.g. recklessness and negligence.
- Mistake of law may be good defense where accused was told officially that his or her act was not criminal.
- Mistake of law is good defense where knowledge of criminality of conduct is element of offense.

CHAPTER 5

Causation

Where a criminal offense includes an actus reus element requiring the prosecution to prove that a particular result occurred, e.g. the death of a victim for homicide offenses, *see* Chapter 12 (Homicide), it usually requires proof as well of the fact that the accused's conduct caused that criminal result.

This causation requirement necessitates proof of both parts of a two-pronged test: (1) that the accused's conduct *actually* caused the criminal result; *and* (2) that the accused's conduct was a *legally sufficient* cause of the criminal result.

Model Penal Code. The Model Penal Code (MPC) follows this general rule. MPC § 2.03(1) provides that "[c]onduct is the cause of a result when: (a) it is an antecedent but for which the result in question would not have occurred; and (b) the relationship between the conduct and result satisfies any additional causal requirements imposed by the Code or by the law defining the offense."

A. ACTUAL CAUSATION

The actual causation prong of the causation test is often called the "but for" requirement. The inquiry is as follows: *but for* the accused's actions, would the criminal result have occurred when it did?

This is not a very demanding test. An accused person who assaulted a victim, leading to her hospitalization and subsequent death is clearly a "but for" cause of the victim's death, for example, even if the victim died from an infection she picked up while hospitalized. But for the assault, the victim wouldn't have been in the hospital where she contracted the fatal infection when she did.

Multiple actors. More than one person can be the actual or but for cause of the same criminal result, even if they act independently. The accused person who assaulted his victim, putting her in the hospital where she died subsequently is a but for cause of her death. But for the assault the victim wouldn't have been in the hospital where she died when she did.

But the but for test includes many more potential defendants in those hypothetical circumstances. The hospital orderly, for example, who negligently wheeled the same victim into an open elevator shaft, leading to her fall and subsequent fatal injuries would also be a but-for cause of the victim's death. But for the orderly's actions, the victim would not have died when she did.

Multiple mortal wounds. If more than one person inflicts an instantly fatal wound on the same victim at the very same time, e.g. each shoots him in the head at point blank range, it could be argued that neither one is the but for cause of death since the victim would have died anyway (at the same time) due to the action of the other. But the law holds otherwise. Each independent but mortal act is deemed to be sufficient to serve as an actual cause of the victim's death. *See, e.g., Burrage v. U.S.*, 571 U.S. 204, 214 (2014) ("[C]ourts have not always required strict but-for causality[.] The most common (though still rare) instance of this occurs when multiple sufficient causes independently, but concurrently, produce a result.").

Where, however, one person seriously assaults a victim but the victim doesn't die immediately, and is ultimately killed by a second person, acting independently, some courts find the first actor not to be the actual cause of the victim's death (although he or she may be guilty of attempted murder) due to the existence of the second person's intervening act. Other courts find both actors to be the actual cause of the victim's death, assuming that both wounds were mortal or hastened the victim's death. *See Burrage v. U.S.*, 571 U.S. 204, 214–16 (2014).

B. LEGAL CAUSATION

In addition to actual (but for) causation, the prosecution must also prove that the relationship between the accused's conduct and the criminal result was legally sufficient to justify criminal culpability. Jurisdictions use a variety of different tests for legal causation.

Legal causation tests. The tort law legal causation test is "proximate cause." A minority of jurisdictions use this same test (or at least this same name) to assess legal causation in criminal law.

But most jurisdictions use more stringent tests than the civil law, requiring a demonstration of a closer causal link than in tort law. This is because a criminal conviction results in the imposition of punishment, including incarceration often, rather than the award of mere economic damages as in tort law.

Such criminal law legal causation tests are often referred to by such names as "efficient cause," "main cause," and "direct cause" tests. But invariably, they include some consideration both of what the actor should have reasonably foreseen might occur when he or she acted, as well as the presence of unforeseeable intervening or supervening causes that may have occurred and led more directly to the ultimate criminal result. The presence of a sufficiently intervening cause is said to "break the causal chain."

MPC "not too remote or accidental" test. MPC § 2.03(2)–(4) provide that: "(2) When purposely or knowingly causing a particular result is an element of an offense, the element is not established if the actual result is not within the purpose or the contemplation of the actor unless: (a) the actual result differs from that designed or contemplated, as the case may be, only in the respect that a different person or different property is injured or affected or that the injury or harm designed or contemplated would have been more serious or more extensive than that caused; or (b) the actual result involves the same kind of injury or harm as that designed or contemplated and is *not too remote or accidental* in its occurrence to have a [just] bearing on the actor's liability or on the gravity of his offense[;] (3) When recklessly or negligently causing a particular result is an element of an offense, the element is not established if the actual result is not within the risk of which the actor is aware or, in the case of negligence, of which he should be aware unless: (a) the actual result differs from the probable result only in the respect that a different person or different property is injured or affected or that the probable injury or harm would have been more serious or more extensive than that caused; or (b) the actual result involves the same kind of injury or harm as the probable result and is *not too remote or accidental* in its occurrence to have a [just] bearing on the actor's liability or on the gravity of his offense[;] (4) When causing a particular result is a material element of an offense for which absolute liability is imposed by law, the element is not established unless the actual result is a probable consequence of the actor's conduct." (emphasis added.)

The key focus of the MPC legal causation test, which has been followed in many jurisdictions, is on the question whether or not the accused's actual conduct was *too remote or accidental* given the criminal result to justify the imposition of criminal sanctions.

This test, like the legal causation tests used in other jurisdictions, necessarily includes some consideration both of what the actor should have reasonably foreseen might occur, as well as the presence of unforeseeable intervening or supervening causes that may have occurred and led more directly to the ultimate criminal result.

Year and a day rule. At common law, the year and a day rule applied. If a death resulted from an actor's conduct, but did not occur within a year and a day from that conduct, no culpability attached for the criminal result. The actor could not be found guilty of homicide (although he or she could be convicted of attempted murder.)

Today, most American jurisdictions have rejected application of the year and a day rule.

Medical treatment. In many jurisdictions, merely negligent medical treatment (ordinary, civil negligence) leading to the death of a victim hospitalized as a result of a prior criminal assault has been held *not* to break the causal chain with respect to the perpetrator of the assault, i.e. he or she is guilty of homicide assuming that the other elements of the offense are met. Gross negligence, on the other hand, has been deemed sufficiently remote or intervening to break the causal chain.

CAUSATION CHECKLIST

A. **Test**—two-pronged: actual (but for) causation + legal causation.

B. **Actual Causation**—but for the accused's actions, would criminal result have occurred when it did?

   1. **Multiple Actors**—more than one person may be actual cause of same criminal result.

   2. **Multiple Mortal Wounds**

      a. **Simultaneous**—actual cause prong met by each actor if more than one independently inflict instantly fatal wounds on same victim at same time.

      b. **Successive**—mixed law whether actual cause prong met where successive mortal wounds or wounds hastening death inflicted by independent actors.

C. **Legal Causation**—stricter test than tort law.

   1. **Tests**—various names; focus on reasonable foreseeability and intervening or supervening causes that "break the causal chain."

   2. **MPC**—was result "too remote or accidental"?

   3. **Year and a Day Rule**—common law rule cutting off culpability after a year and a day largely rejected now.

   4. **Medical Intervening Causes**—gross negligence breaks causal chain; ordinary negligence does not.

ILLUSTRATIVE PROBLEMS

The following problems illustrate how the checklist points help to resolve questions relating to causation.

■ PROBLEM 5.1 ■

Francine DeLauro, a pedestrian, was struck by a car while walking in a crosswalk, and was seriously injured. Joyce Albano was driving the car that hit DeLauro. An ambulance was called to the scene and DeLauro was rushed away immediately in the direction of the nearest hospital.

Unfortunately, all of this occurred in the midst of a terrible thunderstorm and on the way to the hospital, the ambulance was struck by lightning and careened off the road and over an embankment, resulting in the death of three people: DeLauro, the ambulance driver, and the emergency medical technician who was treating DeLauro.

Albano has been charged with homicide in the deaths of all three victims. Is she guilty of these crimes?

Analysis

No.

Albano was not the cause of these three deaths.

As to actual causation, she was in fact the but for cause of all three deaths. But for her actions in hitting DeLauro while she was walking in a crosswalk, DeLauro would not have been in the ambulance and would not have died. Similarly, but for Albano's actions, the ambulance driver and the emergency medical technician would not have been in the ambulance at the place and time that it was struck by lightning and, hence, would not have died.

But actual causation is not enough to establish causal culpability. Was she the legal cause of these deaths? DeLauro's case is trickier. Certainly it can be argued that a driver who runs into a pedestrian could reasonably foresee that the injured pedestrian might subsequently die. But here, DeLauro did not die as a direct result of her injuries from being struck by Albano's car, but rather due to the independent intervening act of the lightning strike. No one can be expected to reasonably foresee where and when lightning will strike. This is, in essence, a classic situation where—in the MPC's terms—DeLauro's death was "too remote or accidental" from Albano's actions to fairly hold her responsible for the ultimate death.

The analysis with respect to the deaths of the ambulance driver and the emergency medical technician is even clearer. Again, no one can be expected to reasonably foresee where and when lightning will strike. Their deaths were clearly "too remote or accidental" from Albano's early actions in striking DeLauro to fairly hold her responsible at criminal law.

■ PROBLEM 5.2 ■

Migdalia Aparicio, in a jealous rage, shot her victim, Tom Jelke, twice in the head, after she saw Jelke flirting with her daughter, Rebecca. When Jelke reached the hospital, his heart was still beating but he had suffered irreversible brain damage and loss of brain function, as evidenced by cessation of breathing and other vital reflexes, unresponsiveness to stimuli, absence of muscle activity, and a flat electroencephalogram. Jelke's family members agreed at his doctors' request to have them discontinue the artificial ventilation that was keeping Jelke's heart beating so that some of his organs could be harvested for transplantation in others.

Aparicio has been charged with first degree murder in the death of Jelke. Her defense counsel argues that the doctors who disconnected Jelke's ventilator were the cause of his death, not Aparicio's act of shooting Jelke.

Is defense counsel correct?

Analysis

No.

Aparicio's actions were the cause of Jelke's death.

The but for analysis is easy here again, as it usually is. But for Aparicio's act of shooting Jelke in the first place, Jelke would not have been in the hospital where his organs were removed.

As to legal causation, in many jurisdictions, we would not even need to consider this question. In those states, death is defined as brain death, the condition in which Jelke reached the hospital. Accordingly, in those states, Jelke would have been considered dead for purposes of the criminal law before his doctors discontinued the use of the artificial ventilator to keep his heart beating and Aparicio was the direct (and only) cause of his death.

However, even assuming that this problem took place in a jurisdiction where someone with a beating heart is still considered to be alive (despite brain death), the doctors' actions here would not be a sufficient intervening cause to break the causal chain between Aparicio's shooting and Jelke's death. It is, of course, reasonably foreseeable—if not altogether likely—that a person shot twice in the head might die. But was it reasonably foreseeable that Aparicio would have died in this particular way, by the doctors' discontinuation of the ventilator? In a case of irreversible brain function, it is reasonably foreseeable that a victim's family might choose to end his life in this fashion. Indeed, whether or not the doctors acted negligently in soliciting and/or effecting this discontinuation, it is not likely that their actions at this stage were the sort of gross negligence that might break the causal chain.

Accordingly, assuming that all of the other elements of first degree murder are met, *see* Chapter 12 (Homicide), Aparicio is guilty as charged.

POINTS TO REMEMBER

- Need both actual (but for) causation + legal causation.
- Multiple actors may be the but for cause of the same criminal result. Where multiple mortal wounds, but for test met if actors acted at same time; mixed law if acted successively.
- Legal causation test stricter in criminal law than tort law.
- Legal causation focuses on reasonable foreseeability of result and presence of intervening causes.
- Common law year and a day rule mostly irrelevant now.
- Ordinary negligence does not break causal chain; gross negligence does.

CHAPTER 6

Accomplice & Vicarious Liability

A. ACCOMPLICE LIABILITY

A person can be found guilty of a crime simply because he or she helped someone else to commit a crime. This type of complicity is usually called accomplice or accessory liability, or aiding and abetting. "The basic view of culpability that animates this doctrine is straightforward: A person may be responsible for a crime he has not personally carried out if he helps another to complete its commission." *Twitter, Inc. v. Taamneh*, 143 S.Ct. 1206, 1220 (2023).

Model Penal Code. Model Penal Code (MPC) § 2.06(1) provides that a "person is guilty of an offense if it is committed by his own conduct or by the conduct of another person for which he is legally accountable, or both."

MPC § 2.06(2)(c) adds that a "person is legally accountable for the conduct of another person" when he or she "is an accomplice of such other person in the commission of the offense."

Common law. "Terms like 'aids and abets' are familiar to the common law, which has long held aiders-and-abettors secondarily liable for the wrongful acts of others." *Twitter, Inc. v. Taamneh*, 143 S.Ct. 1206, 1218 (2023). At common law, there were four categories of participants to a felony: principals in the first degree; principals in the second degree; accessories before the fact; and accessories after the fact:

- Principals in the first degree were people who were present and actually committed the criminal act, e.g. the person who held a gun on a bank teller during a bank robbery.
- Principals in the second degree were the people who were present at the crime scene (actually or

constructively) and assisted in its commission, e.g. a get-away driver.

- Accessories before the fact were persons who aided or encouraged the principals before the crime occurred, but were not present at the crime scene.
- Accessories after the fact offered aid or encouragement after the crime was completed.

The culpability of an accomplice at common law "shadowed" that of the principal. That meant that an accomplice could not be convicted unless or until a principal was convicted of the crime in question. However, a principal in the second degree could be convicted whether or not a principal in the first degree had been convicted previously.

Additionally, any person who aided or encouraged the commission of a misdemeanor was treated as a principal at common law.

Merger of categories. Significantly, these common law distinctions between parties to a crime have been largely abrogated today by statute. With one exception, accessories after the fact, the categories of principal and accessory are said to have "merged."

That means that someone may be convicted of commission of a crime simply by proving the elements of accomplice liability with respect to that crime. In essence, an accomplice is treated as if he or she actually committed (as a principal) the crime that was assisted.

Moreover, as a result of this merger, the culpability of an accessory no longer turns on whether a principal has been convicted previously of the same crime. An accomplice to a crime can be convicted of that crime simply by proving that he or she was an accomplice, regardless of what has happened—if anything—to any principal.

As MPC § 2.06(7) provides, "[a]n accomplice may be convicted on proof of the commission of the offense and of his complicity therein, though the person claimed to have committed the offense has not been prosecuted or convicted or has been convicted of a different offense or degree of offense or has an immunity to prosecution or conviction or has been acquitted."

Notice. Since a person can be convicted of a crime today by proof that he or she was merely an accomplice (rather than a principal), the prosecution must give an accused person adequate pre-trial notice whether it intends to prove at trial that he or she acted as a principal or an accomplice.

Exception: accessories after the fact. The status of accessory after the fact has not merged with any other status. Although accessories *before* the fact are treated like principals, accessories *after* the fact are not.

An accessory after the fact might well be convicted of a separate crime. But that crime must relate to any criminal activity committed after another crime was committed, e.g. obstruction of justice, harboring a fugitive, or receiving stolen property.

Mens rea. To be convicted as an accomplice, an accused must have intended to assist another person in committing a crime and intended that that person actually commit that crime. This mens rea is often established circumstantially.

Mere presence at the scene of a crime is never enough, however, to establish the mens rea of complicity.

Actus reus. To be convicted as an accomplice, an accused must have actively assisted another person in the commission of a crime. Such assistance can be established by the solicitation of another person to commit a crime. *See* Chapter 9 (Solicitation). *See Twitter, Inc. v. Taamneh*, 143 S.Ct. 1206, 1221 (2023): "Criminal law requires that a defendant in some sort associate himself with the venture, that he participate in it as in something that he wishes to bring about, that he seek by his action to make it succeed before he could be held liable. In other words, the defendant has to take some affirmative act with the intent of facilitating the offense's commission. Such intentional participation can come in many forms, including abetting, inducing, encouraging, soliciting, or advising the commission of the offense, such as through words of encouragement or driving the getaway car."

The extent of the accused's assistance is irrelevant. However, unwittingly assisting an undercover agent who is trying to find a criminal (e.g. to sell him narcotics) is not enough in and of itself to establish active assistance. In contrast, assisting a person who is committing a crime (e.g. the drug seller) is enough.

As a general rule, mere physical presence at the scene of a crime is not enough to establish that a criminal act occurred. *Twitter, Inc. v. Taamneh*, 143 S.Ct. 1206, 1221 (2023) ("Not all those present at the commission of a trespass are liable as principals."). Some jurisdictions, however, recognize an exception to this rule where the accused's failure to act to prevent the crime from occurring violates a legal duty to act, e.g. the accused is a minor victim's parent.

Renunciation or withdrawal. The law in most jurisdictions is that an accomplice may not successfully withdraw or renounce his or her criminal intention after a criminal act has already taken place. But this is a defense in a few jurisdictions if it occurs before the criminal act, and the actor keeps the crime from occurring. MPC § 2.06(6) provides for just such a defense where the actor "(i) wholly deprives [the assistance] of effectiveness in the commission of the offense; or (ii) gives timely warning to the law enforcement authorities or otherwise makes proper effort to prevent the commission of the offense."

Scope. In most jurisdictions, an accomplice can be convicted only for those crimes he or she actually intended to assist or could reasonably have foreseen would have resulted from his or her assistance.

Conspiratorial complicity. In many jurisdictions, co-conspirators, *see* Chapter 8 (Conspiracy), are held responsible under the criminal law for the reasonably foreseeable actions of their co-conspirators undertaken in furtherance of the conspiracy. This rule is often called the "*Pinkerton* Doctrine" as it was applied under federal criminal law in *Pinkerton v. U.S.*, 328 U.S. 640 (1946).

Notably, however, "unlike its close cousin conspiracy, aiding and abetting does not require any agreement with the primary wrongdoer to commit wrongful acts, thus eliminating a significant limiting principle." *Twitter, Inc. v. Taamneh*, 143 S.Ct. 1206, 1221 (2023).

B. VICARIOUS LIABILITY

A person may be convicted of a crime vicariously, i.e. on the basis of another person's criminal conduct for which the first person is held responsible by law even though he or she was not directly involved in it.

Model Penal Code. MPC § 2.06(1) provides that a "person is guilty of an offense if it is committed by his own conduct or by the conduct of another person for which he is legally accountable, or both."

MPC § 2.06(2)(b) adds that a "person is legally accountable for the conduct of another person" when he or she "is made accountable for the conduct of such other person by the Code or by the law defining the offense."

Corporate responsibility. Corporations may be held responsible vicariously for the actions of their agents or employees. Many statutes exist imposing such vicarious corporate liability in regulatory matters.

Corporate officers and agents. Corporate officers are not usually held vicariously responsible for the criminal acts of their subordinates unless they were directly involved in the activity. MPC § 2.07(6)(a) provides that "[a] person is legally accountable for any conduct he performs or causes to be performed in the name of the corporation or an unincorporated association or in its behalf to the same extent as if it were performed in his own name or behalf."

Powerlessness defense. The Supreme Court has ruled that corporate officials may be subject to statutory criminal responsibility—including strict and vicarious liability—assuming that they possessed the actual power and control to keep the criminal activity from taking place. *U.S. v. Park*, 421 U.S. 658 (1975). This is called the "powerlessness defense."

MPC § 2.07(6)(b) provides that "[w]henever a duty to act is imposed by law upon a corporation or an unincorporated association, any agent of the corporation or association having primary responsibility for the discharge of the duty is legally accountable for a reckless omission to perform the required act to the same extent as if the duty were imposed by law directly upon himself."

COMPLICITY CHECKLIST

A. **Accomplice Liability**—guilt can be based upon helping someone else commit a crime.

   1. **Common Law**—four categories of relationship to crime.

      a. **Principal in the First Degree**—present and actually committed criminal act.

      b. **Principal in the Second Degree**—present and assisted criminal act.

      c. **Accessory Before the Fact**—aided or encouraged principals before crime completed.

      d. **Accessory After the Fact**—aid or encouragement after crime completed.

      e. **Shadowing**—accessory could not be convicted unless principal convicted.

   2. **Merger**—principals and accessories merged today, except accessories after the fact.

      a. **Accessory Treated like Principal**—if prosecution proves assistance, accessory is guilty as if he or she was principal.

b. **No Shadowing**—accessory can be convicted whether or not principal charged or convicted.

c. **Notice**—prosecution must give notice whether it intends to prove accused acted as principal or accomplice.

d. **Accessory After the Fact**—might be convicted of separate crime, but no merger with principal's offense.

3. **Mens Rea**—intent to assist another person in committing a crime, and intent that that person actually commit that crime.

a. **No Direct Evidence**—mens rea often established circumstantially.

b. **Mere Presence**—mere presence at scene of crime not enough for mens rea.

4. **Actus Reus**—active assistance of another in commission of crime.

a. **Assisting Undercover Agent**—assisting undercover agent not criminal act.

b. **Mere Presence**—mere presence at scene of crime not enough for actus reus.

5. **Renunciation or Withdrawal**—usually not a defense, but is defense in minority jurisdictions where before criminal act and actor keeps crime from occurring.

6. **Scope**—accused can be convicted for crimes intended to assist or could reasonably have foreseen.

7. ***Pinkerton* Doctrine**—conspirators held responsible for reasonably foreseeable actions of co-conspirators undertaken in furtherance of conspiracy.

B. **Vicarious Liability**—criminal conviction may be based upon another person's criminal conduct.

1. **Corporate Responsibility**—where statute on point, corporations may be held responsible vicariously for actions of agents or employees.

2. **Corporate Officers**—corporate officers not usually held vicariously responsible for subordinates' criminal acts unless direct involvement.

3. **Powerlessness Defense**—no vicarious responsibility of corporate officers where no power to keep crime from occurring.

ILLUSTRATIVE PROBLEMS

The following problems illustrate how the checklist points help to resolve questions relating to criminal responsibility based upon accomplice and/or vicarious liability.

■ PROBLEM 6.1 ■

Carter Diaz asked Daniel Estragon to sell him two semi-automatic weapons that Diaz could use to "pull off a bank heist." Estragon sold him the weapons. Diaz and his partner, Zola Prince, then used the weapons in a bank robbery, pointing them at the bank tellers and customers, while stealing money and some of the tellers' and customers' valuables. Subsequently, Prince took some of those valuables—watches and jewelry—to Rudolph Pietrowicz, who agreed to buy them from her for a small fraction of their real value. No questions asked.

Diaz, Estragon, Prince and Pietrowicz were all arrested and charged with bank robbery. Diaz and Prince immediately pled guilty in exchange for reduced sentences and their agreement to cooperate with the prosecution and testify against Estragon and Pietrowicz.

Are Estragon and Pietrowicz guilty of bank robbery?

Analysis

Estragon is guilty of bank robbery, but Pietrowicz is not.

Estragon is an accomplice, an accessory before the fact. He knew about the planned bank robbery. He intended to assist Diaz to commit that very crime. It is irrelevant that he did not know whether or not Diaz was really serious or which bank he intended to rob. And, since the status of accomplice has merged with that of principal, by proving the elements of accomplice liability to this crime, the prosecution can convict Estragon of the substantive offense itself: bank robbery. (Estragon may also be guilty of conspiracy and criminal offenses relating to the unlawful sale of semi-automatic weapons.)

Pietrowicz is not guilty of bank robbery because he is an accomplice after the fact. There is no evidence that he knew about the bank robbery before the fact or offered any assistance at all in planning or executing the robbery. Accordingly, his assistance was limited to helping to help the actual bank robbers to profit from their crime after it occurred. Since the status of accomplice after the fact has not merged with that of principal, Pietrowicz is not guilty of bank robbery. He may, of course, be guilty of another crime based on these facts, likely the crime of receiving stolen property.

Parenthetically, if Diaz or Prince had gone to Pietrowicz before the bank robbery and asked him if he would be willing to purchase some of the stolen valuables they recovered from it after the fact, and he agreed, then he would have been guilty of bank robbery as well. That prior knowledge coupled with his intention to assist (evidenced by his willingness to purchase some of the criminal proceeds) would have made him an accessory before the fact rather than an accessory after the fact and, again, the status of accessory before the fact has merged with that of principal.

■ PROBLEM 6.2 ■

Phyllis told her friend Olivia, both members of a hacking club, that Olivia should try to hack into the software of an autonomous vehicle (self-driving car) "just for fun." She explained to Olivia just how to do it. "Cool!," Olivia said, "I'm going to try it on my neighbor's, Liam's, car!" "Wait!," Phyllis responded, "*Wait!* No . . . no . . . wait! On second thought, you know . . . come on, you really shouldn't try that without Liam's permission." Ignoring that plea, Olivia used the hacking information she got from Phyllis to hack into Liam's autonomous car, allegedly, she told the police later, simply to test the quality of its security system. Liam discovered the intrusion, alerted the police, and Phyllis and Olivia were arrested for the crime of computer hacking ("knowingly accessing any computer, computer system or network without permission"). Olivia took a plea deal to testify against Phyllis, who was tried for this offense as Olivia's accomplice. Phyllis's defense counsel claims that she renounced any intention to assist Olivia in committing this crime. Is that a good defense in this situation?

Analysis

No.

In those jurisdictions where renunciation of a criminal intent to assist someone else in the commission of a crime is a defense, to be effective, the renunciation (or withdrawal) must keep the crime from actually occurring. That didn't happen here. The crime occurred. Hence, even if a renunciation defense existed in this jurisdiction, it would be ineffective as a defense for Phyllis to a charge of being an accomplice to computer hacking.

■ PROBLEM 6.3 ■

Linda Childers knows that Gloria Nixon, who lives nearby, sells narcotics from her apartment. Childers has talked about this fact with other neighbors. It's common knowledge in the neighborhood what Nixon is doing, but Childers has not told the police or anyone else in an official capacity about this.

Tonetta Poole, a police officer working undercover, comes up to Childers on the street and asks her if she knows where Nixon lives. Childers doesn't recognize Poole, knows she's not from the neighborhood, and suspects that Poole is looking for Nixon in order to buy narcotics. But Childers tells Poole where Nixon lives anyway, and Poole goes there and does buy narcotics.

Nixon is arrested and prosecuted for the unlawful sale of narcotics. Can Childers be prosecuted successfully as Nixon's accomplice on the basis of the assistance she rendered in directing Poole to Nixon?

Analysis

No.

Childers lacks both the mens rea and actus reus for accomplice liability. She did not know that Poole was trying to buy narcotics from Nixon, she merely suspected it. And, in any event, there is no evidence that Childers had the intent to assist Nixon in committing the crime of unlawful sale of narcotics, or the intent that Nixon actually commit that crime.

Similarly, Childers did not actively assist Nixon in the commission of this crime. She merely unwittingly assisted an undercover agent who was trying to—and did—find a criminal. That is not enough for accomplice liability.

Of course, if the facts are changed slightly, the answer to this question might change as well. Suppose, for example, that the prosecution could prove that Childers knew that Nixon would pay her some sort of fee if she forwarded customers to her and that is why she directed Poole to Nixon. That's a different case altogether. In that event, both the mens rea (intent to assist) and the actus reus (active assistance of Nixon) of accomplice liability might well be present. And if Childers was culpable as an accomplice, she would then be guilty of the crime of sale of narcotics itself since accomplice and principal culpability have merged.

■ PROBLEM 6.4 ■

Snidely Whiplash is the Chief Executive Officer (CEO) of Bullwinkle Industries (BI). BI manufactures, among other products, a specialty shampoo for the washing and conditioning of human facial hair, Bullwinkle's Beard Balm. One of BI's employees, Nell Fenwick, a chemist, unbeknownst to any of the other employees of BI, changed the chemical formulation of Bullwinkle's Beard Balm so that it could be combined with another BI product, Rocky Road Lip Gloss, to make a powerful explosive.

When Fenwick tried to carry a large quantity of Bullwinkle's Beard Balm and Rocky Road Lip Gloss onto a commercial jet on a domestic flight in order to combine them onboard and blow up the plane in a senseless act of domestic terrorism, she was caught by TSA screening officials, and confessed all of her plans. She was subsequently arrested, prosecuted and convicted for various criminal offenses relating to her criminal acts of attempted terrorism.

Subsequently, BI and Whiplash individually, were charged with violating various criminal provisions of the federal Food, Drug and Cosmetic Act, 21 U.S.C. § 301, et seq., due to the unsafe and adulterated formulation of Bullwinkle's Beard Balm, which had been devised by Fenwick. BI pleaded guilty to these charges and was fined $50,000. Whiplash has pleaded not guilty and faces trial. What are his chances of being found not guilty at trial?

Analysis

His chances are fifty-fifty.

Given an appropriate statute (and there is one under the federal Food, Drug and Cosmetic Act), a corporate officer can be held vicariously responsible for the criminal acts of a subordinate corporate agent or employee. But such vicarious liability cannot attach where the corporate officer can demonstrate that he or she was powerless to prevent the criminal activity from occurring.

The question for a criminal jury then is whether Whiplash was powerless—whether he lacked sufficient control—to prevent Fenwick from reformulating Bullwinkle's Beard Balm in an unsafe and adulterated fashion.

One could imagine that Whiplash would argue, through his defense counsel, that there was no way that he could have discovered that Fenwick was reformulating the product in this crazy fashion. He's not a chemist. He wasn't physically present when all of this occurred. He had no way of assessing or discovering the reformulation. His tasks are administrative, not scientific.

And one could imagine the prosecution arguing in response that Whiplash was in a sufficiently responsible position—he was CEO, after all—that he should have made certain that adequate controls were in place to ensure that such criminal conduct could not take place and that all of BI's product formulations were safe.

Will he be found guilty? Which arguments will the jury accept? It's a toss-up.

POINTS TO REMEMBER

- At common law, there were four parties to a crime: principals in the first degree; principals in the second degree; accessories before the fact; and accessories after the fact.
- At common law, an accessory could not be convicted unless a principal was convicted.
- Today principals and accessories have merged, except accessories after the fact.
- Today, an accessory can be convicted whether or not a principal was charged or convicted.
- Person convicted as an accomplice is treated like a principal.
- Accomplice mens rea is intent to assist and intent that crime be committed.
- Accomplice actus reus is active assistance.
- Mere presence at crime scene is not enough for accomplice mens rea or actus reus.
- Accomplice can be convicted for unintended crimes if he or she reasonably could have foreseen their commission.
- Conspirators can be held responsible for reasonably foreseeable actions of their co-conspirators undertaken in furtherance of conspiracy.
- Convictions may be based on vicarious responsibility where statute exists.
- No vicarious responsibility of corporate officer where powerless to keep crime from occurring.

CHAPTER 7

Attempt

Attempt is one of three common inchoate offenses: attempt; conspiracy; and solicitation. *See* Chapter 8 (Conspiracy) & Chapter 9 (Solicitation). An inchoate offense is a criminal offense committed by a person who is trying to commit another crime (the choate offense).

A. ACTUS REUS

Mere preparation. To satisfy the actus reus element of attempt, a person must be shown to have done something more than to simply engage in "mere preparation" to commit a crime.

How much more? The classic test for the actus reus of attempt focused on the question of how close the actor came to actually completing the criminal offense he or she intended to commit ("proximity tests").

Today, however, following the Model Penal Code (MPC) approach, jurisdictions commonly focus instead on how far the accused went toward completing the intended offense ("substantial step test"). This change in focus—from how close the accused came to a crime to how far the accused went—has resulted in making much more preparatory conduct punishable as attempts.

Proximity tests. Traditionally, attempt actus reus tests were one form or another of a "proximity test." They attempted to assess the closeness or "proximity" of the actor's conduct to accomplishing his or her intended criminal objective.

Different jurisdictions used a number of different variations of verbal formulae in the attempt to gauge such proximity. In England, the proximity test used was originally the "last proximate act" test, which was also adopted early on in some American states. This test was satisfied only when the prosecution proved that the accused had completed the very last act possible before the intended crime would have been completed. This test was difficult to satisfy, left much dangerous activity unpunished and unpunishable, and is no longer used anywhere.

Some of the other proximity tests that have been used are:

- the "physical proximity test" under which the accused must have neared completion of the intended crime;
- the "dangerous proximity test" under which the court considered the gravity and probability of the offense in addition to the nearness of the act to the crime;
- the "indispensable element test" which emphasized the question whether an indispensable aspect of the criminal endeavor remained to be completed;
- the "probable desistance test" which focused on whether the conduct of the accused would result in the intended crime if there was no interruption from an outside source;
- the "abnormal step approach" where the focus was on whether the conduct of the accused went beyond the point where a normal person would have thought better of his or her conduct and desisted;
- and the "res ipsa loquitur" or "unequivocality test" under which the analysis was whether the accused's conduct clearly manifested the intent to commit a crime.

Proximity test is minority view. A minority of states continue to use a proximity test to assess whether or not an accused has met the actus reus element of attempt by taking actions that go beyond mere preparation.

Model Penal Code "substantial step" test. The MPC rejected proximity tests for assessment of the actus reus of attempt. Instead, MPC § 5.01 provides that the actus reus element is met where the accused takes a "substantial step in a course of conduct planned to culminate in his commission of the crime."

Majority view: substantial step. The substantial step test is now the majority rule in American jurisdictions.

It makes actions undertaken in preparation for the commission of a crime criminal attempts well before proximity tests would. This is true because the key question to be asked and answered today is how far did the accused go toward committing a crime, rather than—under a proximity test—how close did he or she get to completing it? The latter inquiry, in fact, is irrelevant under the substantial step test. *See, e.g.*, *United States v. Taylor*, 142 S. Ct. 2015, 2020 (2022) ("A substantial step demands something more than 'mere preparation.' ").

B. MENS REA

The mens rea of attempt is the intent to commit the specific crime that was the actor's criminal objective.

Specific intent. The prosecution cannot establish this element simply by proving that the accused intended to commit some—*any*—criminal act. Rather, the prosecution must establish instead that the accused intended to commit the specific crime for which he or she is being charged as attempting. Such proof is often established circumstantially.

Model Penal Code. MPC § 5.01(1) provides that a "person is guilty of an attempt to commit a crime if, acting with the kind of culpability otherwise required for the commission of the crime, he: (a) purposely engages in conduct that would constitute the crime if the attendant circumstances were as he believes them to be; or (b) when causing a particular result is an element of the crime, does or omits to do anything with the purpose of causing or with the belief that it will cause such result without further conduct on his part; or (c) purposely does or omits to do anything that, under the circumstances as he believes them to be, is an act or omission constituting a substantial step in a course of conduct planned to culminate in his commission of the crime."

Attempted negligence or recklessness. Logically, a person who intends to act recklessly or negligently in order to accomplish a criminal result is actually acting intentionally, i.e. that person knows exactly what he or she is trying to do. Since attempt crimes require proof of the intent to commit a specific crime, most jurisdictions do not recognize the existence of attempt crimes where the mens rea for the offense attempted is recklessness or negligence.

Involuntary manslaughter is a good example. There is no such crime as attempted involuntary manslaughter, a crime which has a mens rea of recklessness or criminal negligence. *See* Chapter 12 (Homicide). Attempt requires the intent to commit the specific crime. If a person intends to kill someone, that's not involuntary manslaughter. Someone intending but failing to kill someone else is guilty of attempted murder instead.

C. LESSER INCLUDED OFFENSE

Attempt is a crime in and of itself, wholly separate from the choate offense that the accused intended and hoped to commit. The actus reus of attempt is significantly different from the actus reus of the choate crime actually intended, as described above, although the mens rea may be the same or different from that required to prove the choate offense.

Ordinarily, when all of the elements of one crime are included within the elements of another crime (which has one or more additional elements), the former crime is considered to be a "lesser included offense" and "merges"—for purposes of sentencing with the latter crime (the "greater offense"). All of the elements of attempt are not included within the choate offense attempted because the actus reus of each offense is different, as described above. Despite that, attempt is nonetheless treated as a "lesser included offense" of the intended choate offense, if that offense actually took place and the accused was convicted of committing it.

Merger. This means that if an accused person is convicted *both* of an attempt to commit a crime and the actual commission of that same crime, the offenses merge. The convicted defendant can only be sentenced for the greater offense, not *both* the greater and the lesser offense (attempt).

D. ABANDONMENT DEFENSE

In order to encourage people who have begun to commit crimes to stop before completion, in most jurisdictions, it is a good defense to an attempt charge that the accused abandoned or renounced his or her criminal objective before committing the substantive crime intended.

This is a significant difference between choate and inchoate offenses: choate offenses cannot be abandoned once committed; inchoate offenses can, in most jurisdictions.

Conditions for abandonment. The abandonment defense is, however, available only under certain specific conditions. MPC § 5.01(4) provides, for example, that "it is an affirmative defense that [the accused] abandoned his effort to commit the crime or otherwise prevented its commission, under circumstances manifesting a complete and voluntary renunciation of his criminal purpose. . . [R]enunciation of criminal purpose is not voluntary if it is motivated, in whole or in part, by circumstances, not present or apparent at the inception of the actor's course of conduct, that increase the probability of detection or apprehension or that make more difficult the accomplishment of the criminal purpose. Renunciation is not complete if it is motivated by a decision to postpone the criminal conduct until a more advantageous time or to transfer the criminal effort to another but similar objective or victim."

In jurisdictions that accept an abandonment defense for attempt crimes, preconditions such as those set out by the MPC are common.

An abandonment must be voluntary and complete to be a good defense.

An abandonment is not voluntary and complete, for example, when a person desists because he or she hears a police siren or sees or hears something else that indicates that there is an increased chance that he or she might be caught.

A good abandonment defense is generally based upon proof of an actor's internal decisions not to persist in criminal conduct. The defense is inapplicable where the abandonment was instead prompted by external changes in the circumstances of the criminal conduct which increased the risks involved or motivated the actor to postpone the conduct until a more propitious time or to target another person.

E. IMPOSSIBILITY DEFENSE

Factual vs. legal impossibility. Courts used to try to distinguish between "factual impossibility" which was not a defense to an attempt crime, and "legal impossibility" which was a defense:

- A factual impossibility was said to exist where the facts present at the time of the attempt, unknown to the person acting, made the commission of the crime intended impossible.
- A legal impossibility was said to exist when a person committed acts which, as a matter of law, simply could not have amounted to the crime charged as the subject of the attempt.

Not a good distinction. The problem was that the same actions could be treated as either a factual or a legal impossibility depending on how one looked at the circumstances. For example, if a person tried to bribe a juror but failed because the individual offered the bribe was not actually a juror, that could be viewed as a factual impossibility as the facts present at the time of the attempt (not a juror), unknown to the person acting, made the commission of the crime intended (bribery) impossible to commit. Viewed as a factual impossibility, this is no defense to an attempt charge.

But the identical facts could just as easily be viewed as a legal impossibility. The person committed acts (trying to bribe a juror) which, as a matter of law, simply could not have amounted to the crime charged as the subject of the attempt (attempted bribery). Viewed as a legal impossibility, this was a defense to an attempt charge.

In essence, whether or not a defense existed was a product of whether one looked to what the actor intended to do (factual impossibility) or instead to what actually occurred (legal impossibility).

Rejection of impossibility defense. The MPC eliminated the impossibility defense altogether in attempt cases. That rejection was subsequently followed by many states in the United States. In those jurisdictions, it is therefore no longer a defense to an attempt charge that a person has committed acts which, as a matter of law, could not have amounted to the crime charged as the subject of the attempt.

ATTEMPT CHECKLIST

A. **Actus Reus**—beyond mere preparation.

   1. **Proximity Tests**—traditional tests focused on how close to crime person got.

   2. **Substantial Step Test**—MPC and majority test focuses on how far actor has gone toward crime.

   3. **Modern Test More Inclusive**—more actions beyond mere preparation are criminal attempts under modern test.

B. **Mens Rea**—intent to commit specific crime that was actor's objective.

   1. **Generalized Criminal Intent**—is not enough.

   2. **No Attempted Recklessness or Negligence Crimes**—attempting to cause a criminal result is intentional conduct.

C. **Merger**—attempt conviction merges with conviction for crime attempted.

D. **Abandonment Defense**—majority recognize attempt defense where person abandoned criminal objective before committing crime intended.

   1. **Voluntary**—not good defense if abandoned due to increased probability of detection or apprehension or greater difficulty.

   2. **Complete**—not good defense if only postponing conduct or switching target.

E. **Impossibility Defense**

   1. **Traditional Defense Existed**—only for legal impossibility; not for factual impossibility.

a. **Factual Impossibility**—facts present, unknown to person acting, made commission of crime intended impossible.

b. **Legal Impossibility**—person committed acts which could not have amounted to crime charged as subject of attempt.

c. **Difference in Focus**—factual impossibility looked to what actor intended to do; legal impossibility looked to what actually occurred.

2. **MPC & Many States Reject**—impossibility not a defense to attempt crimes today in many jurisdictions.

ILLUSTRATIVE PROBLEMS

The following problems illustrate how the checklist points help to resolve questions relating to attempt crimes.

■ PROBLEM 7.1 ■

Daniel Goldsmith, having slept through his alarm clock and discovering that he is very late for work, decides to drive his car to the office even though he knows that all of the tires on the car are bald and that there is a real risk of a blow out.

In fact, that is exactly what happens. Only 4 blocks from home, his left front tire blows out and his car careens out of control and he hits a pedestrian. The pedestrian doesn't die, fortunately, but she is seriously injured.

Is Goldsmith guilty of an attempted homicide crime?

Analysis

No.

Goldsmith certainly may be guilty of a vehicular offense involving a mens rea of negligence or recklessness, but he is not guilty of attempted homicide. First degree murder requires a mens rea of the specific intent to kill someone, *see* Chapter 12 (Homicide), and there is no indication on these facts that Goldsmith set out to kill a pedestrian. As a result, he is not guilty of attempted murder.

Other homicide offenses generally involve some form of gross recklessness or gross negligence as the mens rea, *see* Chapter 12 (Homicide), and hence are not proper subjects for an attempt crime as, by definition, one cannot specifically intend to be reckless or negligent without actually being guilty of acting intentionally.

The irony here is that if the pedestrian that Goldsmith hit had died, Goldsmith could possibly have been found guilty of any homicide offense involving recklessness or negligence, e.g. involuntary manslaughter. But, given the stricter mens rea requirement for attempt crimes, where the victim lived and where he did not actually intend to kill her, he is not guilty of an attempted homicide offense.

■ PROBLEM 7.2 ■

Dierks Swift and Taylor Bentley decide to rob a bank and make their robbery plans with care. Swift visits the bank a couple of times to assess the layout of the teller floor. Bentley purchases stockings for masks to wear and buys some fake guns that they have decided they will try and pass off as real during the robbery.

Everything is all set in their planning, except that when they wake up the morning of the planned robbery, they read in the morning paper that the bank is closed for the day due to an obscure bank holiday. Unfortunately, as they discuss their disappointment at this unexpected change in plans at their local coffee shop, they are overheard by an undercover police officer who sits down at their table and identifies himself as a cop. Bentley, nerves frayed, flatly blurts out: "Hey, this wasn't my idea!" At which point, Swift confesses exactly what they had planned to do, namely rob the bank.

Swift and Bentley are both charged with attempted bank robbery. Are they guilty of this crime?

Analysis

It depends on what jurisdiction they are in. If they are in a (minority) jurisdiction that uses a proximity test to determine whether the actus reus of attempt is satisfied, then, in all probability, they cannot be convicted of attempted bank robbery. They simply did not come close enough to actually completing their plan to satisfy a proximity test.

On the other hand, if they had the misfortune of doing exactly the same thing in a (majority) substantial step jurisdiction, then, in all probability, they can be convicted of attempted bank robbery. Swift's act of "casing" the bank premises was certainly a substantial step. Bentley could likely be convicted as an accomplice, *see* Chapter 6 (Accomplice & Vicarious Liability), and/or she can be convicted in her own right on the basis of the substantial step she took in purchasing masks and fake guns to use in the planned robbery.

■ PROBLEM 7.3 ■

Louis King plans to bake some marijuana brownies for his partner, Cyrus James', thirtieth birthday celebration. This takes place in a state where possession of marijuana is still a crime. Inexperienced in purchasing marijuana, however, King takes a bus to a part of town where he has heard that narcotics are sold on the street and, asking people where he can get some "weed," he ends up buying a baggie containing an ounce of what he is told is "some really good shit" from an Italian hoagie street vendor. In fact, what he actually purchased was not marijuana at all; it was dried oregano.

King took the supposed "marijuana" home, baked it into two trays of brownies, and served it to James and some of James' friends. James remarked that "there's sort of a delicate herbal flavor to these things," to which King responded: "That herb is marijuana, Cyrus. I baked some into the brownies for your birthday!" Unfortunately, one of Fox's friends who was standing right there, Doug Manson, was a Drug Enforcement Agency agent and he immediately seized the brownies and arrested King.

King, of course, cannot be charged with possession of marijuana as there was no marijuana. But can he be convicted successfully for attempted possession of marijuana?

Analysis

In all likelihood, yes.

As to the mens rea of attempt, King had the intent to commit the specific crime of possession of marijuana. As to actus reus, arguably, he came close to accomplishing that criminal goal (the test in a minority proximity jurisdiction), and certainly he took a substantial step toward the criminal conduct as he tried his best to actually purchase marijuana (substantial step test is the majority approach).

Moreover and most important here, in the great majority of jurisdictions, there is no impossibility defense to attempt crimes today. As a result, it is no defense for him to argue (as he traditionally could have) that he only committed acts which, as a matter of law, could not have amounted to the crime charged as the subject of the attempt (possession of marijuana) since he only managed to possess oregano, not marijuana.

■ PROBLEM 7.4 ■

As Linda Soros was walking home late one night from the bus stop, she was grabbed roughly by Bob Parkerman, who pulled her into the bushes and started choking her and ripping at her clothes.

"You know what I want, honey!," Parkerman hissed, "Just let me do what I want and I'll leave you alone after that. Calm down, baby!" Choking, but fighting back as much as she could, Soros gasped: "Stop! Stop! Leave me alone! You don't want me. I'm having my period." Hearing that, Parkerman threw her to the ground, turned on his heel and growled at her: "Next time, baby!" Then he stomped away.

Is Parkerman guilty of attempted rape? Does it make any difference in your analysis that Soros was not really having her period when she said that?

Analysis

Parkerman is guilty of attempted rape. His intent to commit the specific offense of rape was clear from his actions and words. *See* Chapter 11 (Sex Crimes). And whatever actus reus test the jurisdiction uses, it was satisfied here. If it uses the proximity test, Parkerman certainly came dangerously close to completing the sexual assault. If it uses the substantial step test, his acts of grabbing her and ripping off some of her clothes clearly satisfies that test.

The key question is whether or not he can make a good defense of abandonment here. But, even assuming this jurisdiction accepts the existence of this defense to attempt crimes, he cannot satisfy the requirements that such withdrawal be both voluntary and complete. Here, it was neither.

It was arguably not voluntary as he did not desist due strictly to his own internal decision not to continue his criminal conduct, but rather because he was prompted by an unanticipated external change in the circumstances (she told him she was having her period and that made commission of the criminal offense less desirable to him). And his withdrawal and desistance was clearly not complete here. Parkerman made it clear that he would try it again ("Next time, baby!").

The fact that Soros may have made up the fact that she was having a period when she was not is irrelevant. The key to the abandonment defense is what circumstances (internal? external?) prompt the accused to desist, not whether whatever was said to him was true or not.

Parkerman is clearly guilty of the crime of attempted rape.

POINTS TO REMEMBER

- A person must go beyond mere preparation to commit an attempt.

- Actus reus test for attempt has shifted from proximity to substantial step analysis.
- More pre-crime conduct is criminalized as attempt under substantial step test.
- Attempt mens rea is intent to commit the specific crime charged as subject of the attempt.
- Attempt conviction merges with conviction for crime attempted.
- Majority recognize abandonment defense for attempt where voluntary and complete.
- Factual impossibility was traditionally no defense to attempt but legal impossibility was a defense.
- Modern view: impossibility is never a defense.

CHAPTER 8

Conspiracy

Conspiracy is one of three common inchoate offenses: attempt; conspiracy; and solicitation. *See* Chapter 7 (Attempt) & Chapter 9 (Solicitation). An inchoate offense is a criminal offense committed by a person who is trying to commit another crime (the choate offense).

Double inchoates. Most jurisdictions do not permit a conviction for a conspiracy to commit an attempt (another inchoate offense). The reason is that—logically—no one would agree with another person to commit an unsuccessful criminal act.

Criticism. Some law professors and judges argue that conspiracy should not be a crime as it often overlaps with attempt and solicitation, and with completion of the offense that was the aim of the conspiratorial agreement. Many commentators also argue that the "sweep" of the conspiracy offense is too broad, netting relatively minor players and treating them as equal co-conspirators with criminals whose culpability is much greater.

Majority have conspiracy statutes. Nonetheless, conspiracy remains a crime in most jurisdictions. A few jurisdictions do not criminalize it, however. A few limit conspiracy to agreements to commit only specified, particularly serious crimes. Where a conspiracy offense applies to an agreement to commit *any* criminal offense (which is the case in most states), that is termed a "general" conspiracy statute.

Co-conspirator hearsay exception. Prosecutors receive an unusual benefit in prosecuting conspiracy cases as compared with other criminal prosecutions since there is an exception to the hearsay rule for statements made by co-conspirators in furtherance of the conspiracy. Such otherwise inadmissible hearsay can come into evidence.

A. UNILATERAL-BILATERAL APPROACH

Classic view: bilateral. Traditionally, a conspiracy consisted of an agreement between two or more persons to commit an unlawful act or a lawful act by unlawful means. This is called a "bilateral" approach to conspiracy because at least two people must actually agree in order to have a conspiracy.

Wharton's rule. In a bilateral jurisdiction, "Wharton's Rule" provides however that two people may not be convicted of conspiracy where they have agreed to commit a crime that necessarily requires the participation of each of them, e.g. a conspiracy to commit bigamy or incest.

Wharton's Rule is inapplicable, however, when the conspiracy involves the cooperation of a greater number of persons than is required for commission of the substantive offense or if the conspirators are not necessary parties to the offense.

Modern view: unilateral. Today, following the Model Penal Code (MPC) approach, MPC § 5.03(1), most jurisdictions have adopted instead a "unilateral" approach to conspiracy.

In unilateral jurisdictions, the act of a single individual who believes that he or she is agreeing with another person to commit a crime is sufficient to establish a conspiracy. There need be no "meeting of the minds." Rather, a person is guilty of being a conspirator under the unilateral approach even if his or her co-conspirator is never found or identified, is not charged, or is acquitted.

Undercover agents. If a person agrees with an undercover agent to commit a crime, that act of agreement is sufficient to establish a conspiracy under the unilateral approach, but it is not under the bilateral approach.

Corporations. A corporation—acting through its employees or agents—may be a party to a criminal conspiracy with another person or another corporation. Two or more agents or employees of the same corporation may also—through their conspiratorial acts—create a criminal conspiracy.

B. MENS REA

Basic rule. The mens rea of conspiracy requires proof of both the intent to agree with another person to commit a crime, and the intent to commit the crime itself.

Inapplicable to recklessness and negligence. In most jurisdictions, a person cannot be found guilty of conspiring to commit a crime that involves a mens rea of recklessness or negligence. This is true since, logically, no one can agree to act unintentionally without thereby acting intentionally.

Mere knowledge is not enough. The mens rea of conspiracy is not established simply by showing that an accused person knew that someone else intended to commit a crime. Mere knowledge of impending criminality is not enough to make out a conspiracy.

Rather, further proof of an intention to join in the conspiratorial conduct is needed in order to establish the mens rea of conspiracy. That further proof can be entirely circumstantial, e.g. the accused knew of the criminal conduct and profited from it as well.

C. ACTUS REUS: AGREEMENT

The actus reus of conspiracy is *not* the criminal act that the conspirators intend to accomplish though their conspiracy, but it is instead the act of agreeing with someone else to commit the crime.

It is seldom possible to establish the existence of such an agreement expressly through the presentation of direct evidence. Rather, a conspiratorial agreement is most often found to exist implicitly, established circumstantially through proof of the concerted activities of the alleged co-conspirators.

Multiple conspiracies or conspiracies with multiple objectives. Since the actus reus of conspiracy is the conspiratorial agreement itself not the criminal act contemplated, the number of conspiracies committed is determined by the number of separate conspiratorial agreements. *See Braverman v. U.S.*, 317 U.S. 49 (1942).

As a result, if conspirators make only one agreement to commit a number of crimes, only one conspiracy exists. Such an agreement could, however, be a continuing agreement. But where a conspirator is a party to a number of separate agreements to commit crimes, multiple conspiracies exist.

Merger. In a majority of jurisdictions, a conspiracy conviction does not merge with conviction for the crime which was the object of the conspiracy, i.e. a defendant can be convicted of and sentenced for both.

However, in many jurisdictions, convictions of multiple inchoate offenses aimed at accomplishing the very same crime do merge. *See* MPC § 5.05(3) ("A person may not be convicted of more than one [attempt, conspiracy or solicitation] designed to commit or to culminate in the commission of the same crime.").

D. OVERT ACT

Majority requirement. In a majority of jurisdictions, establishing the existence of a conspiracy also requires proof by the prosecution of an "overt act" on the part of any one of the conspirators.

An overt act is not the conspiratorial agreement necessary to establish a conspiracy. The overt act must be proved *in addition to* the conspiratorial agreement.

Generally, very little needs to be shown to establish an overt act. The purchase of stockings by one conspirator to be used as masks in a robbery is enough to establish an overt act, for example.

E. DURATION, RENUNCIATION & WITHDRAWAL

Duration. Generally, abandonment of a conspiracy is presumed if none of the conspirators commits an overt act in furtherance of the conspiratorial objective prior to the running of an applicable statute of limitations. However, even if only one conspirator acts within the limitations period, the conspiracy is not abandoned as to all of the conspirators.

Majority: renunciation defense. If the criminal act which is the target of the conspiracy has not yet been completed, most jurisdictions permit a conspirator to defend against a conspiracy charge by proving that he or she renounced his or her conspiratorial intent and withdrew from the conspiracy.

But, to be effective, such a renunciation and withdrawal must be voluntary and complete and the person must "thwart" the commission of the conspiracy. Thwarting can be accomplished by communicating withdrawal to the other conspirators and dissuading them from accomplishing the intended offense. Or the person seeking to withdraw may thwart the conspiracy by assisting law enforcement in preventing the commission of the crime by the remaining co-conspirators.

Voluntary withdrawal. A withdrawal is not voluntary if a conspirator stops conspiring to commit a crime simply because he or she believes that there is an increased risk of being caught by the police.

Complete withdrawal. A withdrawal is not complete if a conspirator stops conspiring to commit one criminal objective while continuing to try and accomplish another criminal objective.

F. ACTS OF CO-CONSPIRATORS

In many jurisdictions, co-conspirators are held responsible under the criminal law for the reasonably foreseeable actions of their co-conspirators undertaken in furtherance of the conspiracy. This rule is often called the "*Pinkerton* Doctrine" as it was applied under federal criminal law in *Pinkerton v. U.S.*, 328 U.S. 640 (1946). *See also* Chapter 6 (Accomplice & Vicarious Liability).

G. CHAIN, WHEEL & SPOKE CONSPIRACIES

Unknown co-conspirators and "chains." You do not need to know who your co-conspirators are in order to have a conspiracy with them. A person who knows that other persons are involved in a conspiracy, even though he or she does not know their identity, is nonetheless a co-conspirator with them. *See, e.g.*, MPC § 5.03(2) ("If a person . . . knows that a person with whom he conspires to commit a crime has conspired with another person or persons to commit the same crime, he is guilty of conspiring with such other person or persons, whether or not he knows their identity. . .").

A conspiracy where someone is deemed to be a co-conspirator with other co-conspirators (known or unknown) up and/or "down the line" from that person, e.g. in a narcotics distribution scheme, is sometimes called a "chain" conspiracy.

"Wheel" and "spoke" conspiracies. A "wheel" conspiracy is one where separate, smaller conspiracies are deemed to be part of a larger conspiracy due to the inclusion of a common co-conspirator (the "hub"). Members of these smaller conspiracies (often "chains" and, in this setting, sometimes called "spokes") can be convicted of the larger one (the "wheel") if it can be proved that they knew of the existence of the other conspiracy or conspirators.

H. RICO

In federal criminal law, the "Racketeer Influenced and Corrupt Organizations Act," 18 U.S.C. §§ 1961–1968, usually called "RICO" for short, also criminalizes conspiracies to participate in a "pattern" of "racketeering activity." A number of states have similar state versions of RICO, sometimes called "baby RICOs."

CONSPIRACY CHECKLIST

A. **In General**—majority have conspiracy statutes, although controversial crime.

   1. **Double Inchoates**—cannot conspire to attempt or solicit.

   2. **Hearsay Exception**—hearsay statements of co-conspirators in furtherance of conspiracy may come into evidence.

B. **Unilateral or Bilateral Conspiracies**—unilateral approach is more inclusive.

   1. **Bilateral**—traditional view: two or more persons must agree to commit unlawful act or lawful act by unlawful means.

      a. ***Wharton's* Rule**—two people cannot be conspirators where they agree to commit crime that necessarily requires participation of both, unless more people involved.

      b. **Undercover Agents**—cannot have conspiracy with undercover agent in bilateral jurisdiction.

   2. **Unilateral**—now majority rule: one person may be conspirator if believes agreeing with another to commit crime.

      a. **Undercover Agents**—can have conspiracy with undercover agent in unilateral jurisdiction.

      b. **Co-Conspirator Status**—person is conspirator under unilateral approach even if co-conspirator is never found or identified, not charged, or acquitted.

C. **Mens Rea**—intent to agree with another to commit crime and intent to commit that crime.

   1. **Recklessness & Negligence**—no conspiracy to commit crime with mens rea of recklessness or negligence.

   2. **Mere Knowledge Not Enough**—mens rea not established simply by showing accused person knew someone else intended to commit crime.

D. **Actus Reus**—agreement with another person to commit crime (can be established circumstantially); plus, in many jurisdictions, overt act in furtherance of conspiracy required.

   1. **Number**—number of conspiracies is determined by number of agreements to commit crimes.

      a. **Multiple Objectives**—one conspiratorial agreement may have multiple criminal objectives.

      b. **Continuing Agreement**—conspiratorial agreement may continue over time.

   2. **Merger**

      a. **Conspiracy & Target Crime**—majority rule: conspiracy conviction does not merge with conviction for crime which was object of conspiracy.

b. **Multiple Inchoates**—convictions of multiple inchoates aimed at same target crime often do merge by statute.

E. **Overt Act**—act in furtherance of conspiracy by any conspirator; not the same as conspiratorial agreement.

F. **Duration**—abandonment of conspiracy presumed where no overt act within statutory limitations period.

G. **Renunciation & Withdrawal**—good defense to conspiracy in majority of jurisdictions.

1. **Voluntary**—withdrawal must be voluntary and not based on belief of increased risk of being caught by police.

2. **Complete**—withdrawal must be complete; cannot stop conspiring on one criminal objective while continuing another.

3. **Thwarting Crime**—person withdrawing must prevent commission of crime; can be accomplished by assisting police in preventing crime by co-conspirators.

H. **Scope of Conspiracies**—can conspire with unknown persons.

1. **Chains**—conspiracy where someone conspires with others up or down the line from him or her.

2. **Wheels & Spokes**—separate conspiracies (spokes) can be part of larger conspiracy where common co-conspirator (hub) and conspirators knew of existence of other conspiracy or conspirators.

ILLUSTRATIVE PROBLEMS

The following problems illustrate how the checklist points help to resolve questions relating to conspiracy.

■ PROBLEM 8.1 ■

Karl Stern asks his friend, Pamela Matthews, if she will help him by transporting some crack cocaine from her residence in Pittsburgh to a friend of his who lives in a Chicago suburb. Matthews says she'll think about it, but she ultimately decides instead to contact the Pittsburgh police and tell them all about Stern's request.

The police recruit Matthews to assist them in apprehending Stern with the narcotics. Matthews then tells Stern that she will help him. He gives her the crack cocaine to deliver while she is wearing a hidden microphone and the police are monitoring the transaction.

Matthews turns the cocaine right over to the police, and Stern is immediately arrested.

Is Stern guilty of conspiracy to distribute cocaine?

Analysis

Assuming that Pennsylvania has a conspiracy statute (it does in fact), the answer to this question depends on whether Pennsylvania is a bilateral or unilateral conspiracy jurisdiction. (In actual fact, Pennsylvania is unilateral.)

In a bilateral jurisdiction, there is no conspiracy on these facts because there was no actual agreement between two or more persons as Matthews was only feigning agreement. Of course, Stern could still be prosecuted for substantive (choate) narcotics offenses, e.g. possession, distribution, etc.

In a unilateral jurisdiction, in contrast, Stern could be found guilty of conspiracy to distribute narcotics. He had the requisite mens rea, the intent to agree and the intent to commit the target offense, distribution of cocaine. The actus reus of conspiracy, an agreement existed as well on Stern's part, despite the fact that Matthews was simply feigning her agreement. Moreover, an overt act was clearly present when Stern gave the crack cocaine to Matthews for her to deliver to Chicago.

■ PROBLEM 8.2 ■

Min Huifen, Fong Lee and Michael Yang have spent two weeks planning to commit a bank robbery. They have acquired guns and have entered the target bank several times on scouting trips to see where the security guard and security cameras are located. Huifen has second thoughts, however, and tells Lee and Yang that she is no longer going to be involved in the robbery. After threatening her with bodily harm if she reveals their plans to anyone else, Lee and Yang nonetheless decide to go ahead with the robbery without Huifen's participation.

One week later, Lee and Yang enter the bank, prepared to rob it. However, as they are entering, Lee notices immediately that there is a new security guard on duty and that he is much younger and physically fit than the security guard who had been in the bank on the previous occasions when they had scouted the premises. That fact gives Lee serious concern, enough concern that he changes his mind about going through with the robbery, and turns right around and leaves the bank. He never pulled out his gun. The actual robbery never began.

But Yang is undaunted. Even though he watched Lee leave the bank, he continues on to a teller's window, pulls out his gun and points it at the teller, and hands over a threatening note, demanding bags of cash. The teller complies, handing over stacks of 20-dollar bills, but at the same time, activating a silent alarm button. As Yang leaves the bank with the cash, he is immediately arrested by police officers who are waiting outside the bank doors, alerted by the alarm.

Are Huifen, Lee, and Yang guilty of conspiracy to commit bank robbery?

Analysis

Yes.

First of all, a conspiracy existed. Before either Huifen or Lee made any attempt to withdraw from the planned robbery, a conspiracy existed. All three had the appropriate mens rea. They intended to—and did—agree to rob the bank and they intended for the bank robbery to be achieved. Prior to the attempted withdrawals, the act of agreement clearly existed as well. Furthermore, their various planning activities, including acquiring guns and scouting the bank, satisfied easily any overt act requirement that this jurisdiction might require.

The key question here is whether Huifen or Lee have good renunciation and withdrawal defenses on these facts, assuming that this scenario occurred in a jurisdiction that recognizes such a defense. Huifen likely does not have a good defense. Although her withdrawal was apparently voluntary and complete, she did not thwart the commission of the bank robbery by the remaining co-conspirators. The fact that she was threatened by the other two if she "spilled the beans" is of no legal consequence.

Lee also does not likely have a valid withdrawal defense for the same reason, but also because his withdrawal would not be considered to be voluntary. He desisted not because he had some sort of internal change of heart about going ahead with this criminal venture, but rather because external events—the presence of a more threatening and intimidating security guard—led him to believe that there was an increased chance of his being hurt or apprehended in the process of committing this crime.

Parenthetically, if the facts were different and if Huifen and Lee did have good withdrawal defenses and Yang realized that both of them had fully withdrawn from the robbery attempt, that might affect Yang's culpability as well. If these events occurred in a bilateral conspiracy jurisdiction where two or more conspirators are required (unlike in a unilateral jurisdiction), the fact that there was only one remaining robber after two successful withdrawals would make a conspiracy conviction untenable as there was no remaining confederate with whom Yang could have conspired.

Indeed, even in a unilateral jurisdiction, if Huifen and Lee successfully withdrew prior to Yang's actions in the bank and he realized as much, it might well be argued that Yang was no longer even attempting to agree with another person to commit this crime. Hence, a conspiracy conviction could not stand even in a unilateral jurisdiction, again, assuming a change in the facts.

Of course, in either a bilateral or unilateral jurisdiction, Yang could still be convicted of the target (choate) offense itself—bank robbery—no matter what would have or could have happened with respect to a conspiracy prosecution.

POINTS TO REMEMBER

- In bilateral jurisdictions, two or more persons must actually conspire to have a conspiracy.
- In unilateral jurisdictions, one person can conspire if he or she believes there is an agreement with another person to commit a crime.
- Conspiracy mens rea is intent to agree with another to commit a crime and intent to commit that crime.
- There is no conspiracy to commit a crime with mens rea of recklessness or negligence.
- Mere knowledge that someone intends to commit a crime is not enough to make someone a conspirator.
- Conspiracy actus reus is agreement with another person to commit a crime.
- A conspirator can conspire with persons he or she does not know.
- The number of conspiracies is determined by the number of agreements to commit crimes.
- A single conspiratorial agreement can have multiple criminal objectives.
- A conspiracy conviction does not merge with conviction of a crime which was an object of conspiracy.
- Some conspiracy statutes also require proof of an overt act in furtherance of conspiracy.
- Conspiracy is still ongoing if overt act within statutory limitations period.

- Renunciation and withdrawal defense available if voluntary and complete and person withdrawing provides assistance to police to prevent the crime.

CHAPTER 9

Solicitation

Solicitation is one of three common inchoate offenses: attempt; conspiracy; and solicitation. *See* Chapter 7 (Attempt) & Chapter 8 (Conspiracy). An inchoate offense is a criminal offense committed by a person who is trying to commit another crime (the choate offense).

Majority have general solicitation statutes. Some commentators have argued that solicitation should not be a crime as it criminalizes conduct at too early a preparatory stage where there is not yet any significant social danger. Despite this criticism, most jurisdictions, following the lead of the Model Penal Code (MPC), have made solicitation a crime with respect to *any* target crime. A solicitation offense applicable to any crime is a "general" solicitation statute.

Some jurisdictions, a minority, however, limit the solicitation offense to the solicitation only of specific crimes—e.g. murder and prostitution—or to serious felonies.

Relationship to complicity. In many jurisdictions, solicitation is not only a separate criminal offense, but it is also one way to establish a person's accomplice liability for commission of the substantive (choate) offense if that offense is committed subsequently by the person solicited. *See* Chapter 6 (Accomplice & Vicarious Liability).

Relationship to attempt. There is mixed law on the question whether or not the act of solicitation alone can constitute an attempt to commit the crime solicited. *See* Chapter 7 (Attempt).

In any event, in many jurisdictions, convictions of multiple inchoate offenses aimed at accomplishing the very same crime merge. *See* MPC § 5.05(3) ("A person may not be convicted of more than one [attempt, conspiracy or solicitation] designed to commit or to culminate in the commission of the same crime.").

A. MENS REA

The mens rea of solicitation is the intent to promote or facilitate the commission of a specific crime by another person who is solicited to commit it.

B. ACTUS REUS

The actus reus of solicitation is commanding, encouraging, or requesting another person to commit a specific crime. Neither the solicitor nor the person being solicited needs to take any action in furtherance of the targeted crime in order for the solicitation to be complete. A person's conduct is not solicitation, however, where it is consists only of obviously hollow threats, joking, or bragging.

Nor is it solicitation to simply express one's approval of another person's criminal intentions. But the crime of solicitation can be committed where a person does not personally initiate discussion of the commission of a crime, but nonetheless expressly encourages someone else who has already decided to commit it to do so.

Relationship to conspiracy. The act element of solicitation includes conduct that falls short of the conduct necessary—a conspiratorial agreement—to establish a criminal conspiracy.

However, if the person solicited agrees to commit the criminal act solicited, then a conspiracy exists. *See* Chapter 8 (Conspiracy).

Impossibility. It is not a defense that the person being solicited could not or would not commit the crime for which he or she was solicited.

Similarly, it does not matter whether or not the criminal act solicited actually took place or not, or even whether the person solicited ever took any steps to accomplish it.

C. CONSTITUTIONAL CONCERNS

Obviously, the act of solicitation involves communicative activity, usually speech (and sometimes writing or nonverbal conduct). The constitutional guarantee of free speech in the First Amendment does not, however, prevent the government from criminalizing speech advocating the use of force or violations of the law where such advocacy "is directed to inciting or producing imminent lawless action and is likely to incite or produce such action." *Brandenburg v. Ohio*, 395 U.S. 444, 447 (1969). *See also Packingham v. North Carolina*, 582 U.S. 98, 107 (2017) ("Specific criminal acts are not protected speech even if speech is the means for their commission.").

D. RENUNCIATION AND ABANDONMENT

After a criminal solicitation has occurred, some jurisdictions (and the MPC) permit a person to defend against a solicitation charge by proving that he or she completely and voluntarily renounced his or her original criminal intention and thereafter prevented the commission of the crime by the person solicited. This renunciation defense is similar to that recognized for the inchoate offense of conspiracy. *See* Chapter 8 (Conspiracy).

Voluntary renunciation. A renunciation is not voluntary if a person acts simply because he or she believes that there is now an increased risk of being caught by the police.

Complete renunciation. A renunciation is not complete if the person making it abandons the solicitation of one criminal objective while continuing to solicit the accomplishment of another criminal objective.

SOLICITATION CHECKLIST

A. **In General**—majority have solicitation statutes, although controversial crime.

   1. **General vs. Specific**—some statutes criminalize soliciting any crime; some only specific crimes.

   2. **Accomplice**—if crime solicited occurs, solicitor is also accomplice.

B. **Mens Rea**—intent to promote or facilitate commission of specific crime by another person.

C. **Actus Reus**—commanding, encouraging, or requesting another person to commit specific crime.

   1. **No Action Necessary**—neither party need act toward completing targeted crime.

   2. **Not Mere Threats or Jokes**—must be more than that, but less than conspiratorial agreement.

   3. **Mere Approval of Another's Criminal Intention Not Enough**—but can solicit by expressly encouraging person who has already decided to commit crime.

   4. **Conspiracy**—if solicitation results in person solicited agreeing to commit the crime solicited, conspiracy exists.

5. **Impossibility**—irrelevant what person being solicited did or whether crime solicited occurred.

D. **Renunciation and Withdrawal**—good defense to solicitation in some jurisdictions.

1. **Voluntary**—withdrawal must be voluntary and not based on belief of increased risk of being caught by police.
2. **Complete**—withdrawal must be complete; cannot abandon one criminal objective while continuing to solicit another.
3. **Preventing Crime**—person withdrawing must prevent commission of crime by person solicited.

ILLUSTRATIVE PROBLEMS

The following problems illustrate how the checklist points help to resolve questions relating to solicitation.

■ PROBLEM 9.1 ■

Hugh Grant approached a woman loitering on a street corner late at night who he assumed was a prostitute and asked her to have sexual relations with him for money. She bargained with him about the amount of money that he would pay her and what she would do for it, but ultimately an agreement was reached. Unfortunately for Grant, it turned out that she was actually an undercover agent posing as a prostitute. As he was walking away with her toward his car, she removed a badge from her clothing and placed him under arrest.

Was Grant guilty of soliciting someone to commit acts of prostitution?

Analysis

Yes.

Assuming both that prostitution is a crime in the jurisdiction where these actions occurred (as it is in the great majority of American jurisdictions) and assuming further that this jurisdiction has a general solicitation statute or a specific solicitation statute applying to prostitution, Grant clearly intended to facilitate the commission of a specific crime—prostitution—by another person who he solicited to commit it. Furthermore, he requested that other person to commit that specific crime. The elements of criminal solicitation are, accordingly, present on these facts. Moreover, there is no indication in these facts that he was joking when he made this request.

It is irrelevant, additionally, that the person solicited did not really intend to commit the crime solicited.

It is also irrelevant that the crime solicited—prostitution—did not actually occur.

Parenthetically, since the undercover agent and Grant did agree to commit a crime, this conduct would also constitute a conspiracy to commit prostitution in a unilateral conspiracy jurisdiction. In a bilateral conspiracy jurisdiction, it would not be enough to establish a conspiracy, as there were not two actual co-conspirators (since the undercover agent was not really a prostitute). *See* Chapter 8 (Conspiracy).

■ PROBLEM 9.2 ■

Zooey Althaus was sitting at a bar one night, talking with her friends, complaining about her partner, when she was overheard by other patrons sitting nearby, yelling to her friends: "She cheated on me again. Again! Which of you will help me kill her? Come on. You know she deserves it. Which of you will kill her for me?"

Althaus' friends kept laughing and talking with her and each other after hearing this, and no one took any steps aimed at harming Althaus' partner, or anyone else.

Is Althaus guilty of the crime of soliciting her friends to murder her partner?

Analysis

No.

It is not likely from these facts that Althaus really had the requisite mens rea of actually promoting or facilitating the murder of her partner by her friends. It also appears clear from all of the circumstances that she did not really request her friends to kill her partner in a serious vein. A person's conduct does not constitute solicitation where it is consists only of obviously hollow threats or joking.

POINTS TO REMEMBER

- If solicited crime occurs, solicitor is also an accomplice.
- Solicitation mens rea is intent to promote or facilitate specific crime by another person.
- Solicitation actus reus is commanding, encouraging, or requesting another person to commit specific crime.

- Neither party needs to take any action toward completing the targeted crime to make out solicitation.
- Solicitation can occur by encouraging someone already planning to commit a crime.
- Conspiracy exists where solicitation results in commission of crime by person solicited.
- Irrelevant what person being solicited did or whether crime solicited occurred.
- Solicitation can be criminal only where it is likely to result in imminent commission of crime.
- Renunciation and withdrawal defense available only if voluntary and complete and prevention of crime.

CHAPTER 10

Assault

Under the common law, assault and battery were separate and distinct crimes. Today, following the lead of the Model Penal Code (MPC), most jurisdictions have merged these separate crimes into one simple assault offense.

Most states have enacted more serious aggravated assault crimes as well. Moreover, assaultive conduct is often one element of even more serious crimes. *See, e.g.,* Chapters 12 (Homicide) and Chapter 11 (Sex Crimes).

A. TRADITIONAL ASSAULT CRIMES

1. Battery

At common law (and in some jurisdictions still today), a person committed the crime of battery by intentionally touching another person against that person's will, thereby injuring him or her.

A battery could also be committed by a non-injurious act of "offensive touching." *See, e.g., Johnson v. U.S.*, 559 U.S. 133, 139 (2010) ("[T]he common-law crime of battery . . . consisted of the intentional application of unlawful force against the person of another. The common law held this element of 'force' to be satisfied by even the slightest offensive touching."). This form of battery usually had a sexual component to it, e.g. touching someone's genitals or a female's breasts. Today, this notion of offensive touching is more commonly criminalized as a separate sexual offense, e.g., indecent contact or indecent assault. *See* Chapter 11 (Sex Crimes).

2. Assault

At common law (and in some jurisdictions still today), a person committed a criminal assault where he or she intentionally placed another person in actual and reasonable fear of an imminent battery.

Assault—unlike battery—included a person's actions intended only to scare or frighten another person, even if no actual touching or any sort of physical contact ever occurred or was intended to occur. Common law assault is often referred to as an attempted battery.

To prove an assault, the prosecution does not need to prove that the victim was actually in physical danger. A victim's reasonable fear of an unlawful touching is enough to establish assault. In some jurisdictions, however, such reasonable fear cannot be established solely by verbal threats.

Attempted assault. Because the crime of assault has been treated commonly as an attempted battery, most jurisdictions have concluded that the crime of attempted assault does not exist since an attempt crime (attempted battery) is already included within the definition of assault itself.

B. MERGER: SIMPLE ASSAULT

Most jurisdictions today have "merged" the elements of the separate common law crimes of assault and battery into a single simple assault crime.

By "merger," what is meant is that simple assault can now be established by proving *either* the elements of the former battery offense *or* the elements of the former assault offense. As a result, no separate battery offense is needed. Put another way, the crime of assault was broadened to include the common law crime of battery (except for offensive touching which is mostly treated as a sex crime, as noted above).

Accordingly, assault today is established where a person *either* intentionally places another person in actual and reasonable fear of an imminent battery *or* intentionally commits a battery.

Consent as a defense. The assault victim's consent is a valid justification defense with respect to some, but not all, assaultive conduct. *See* Chapter 14 (Justification Defenses).

Model Penal Code. MPC § 211.1(1) merges the common law crimes of assault and battery a bit differently, providing as follows: "A person is guilty of assault if he: (a) attempts to cause or purposely, knowingly or recklessly causes bodily injury to another; or (b) negligently causes bodily injury to another with a deadly weapon; or (c) attempts by physical menace to put another in fear of imminent serious bodily injury."

"Bodily injury," is defined in MPC § 210.0(2) as "physical pain, illness or any impairment of physical condition."

C. AGGRAVATED ASSAULT

Most jurisdictions have created additional assault statutes that punish more severely assaultive conduct that is deemed to be more violent or more serious than simple assault (which is a merger of common law assault and common law battery, as discussed). Often simple assault is treated as a misdemeanor and aggravated assault as a felony.

Wide variety. There are a wide variety of different types of aggravated assault statutes. Some apply, for example, to assaults which result in more serious injuries than are contemplated by the crime of simple assault.

Additionally, some other aggravated assault statutes punish assaults which are committed upon a particular category of victims, such as children, the elderly, teachers, police officers, or firemen. Still other aggravated assault statutes punish more severely assaults that are predicates to more serious criminal acts, e.g. assault with intent to rape or assault with intent to murder. And, as yet another example, some aggravated assault statutes punish more severely assaults that are committed in a particular way, e.g. while the perpetrator was carrying a gun or driving a vehicle (assault with a deadly weapon or vehicular assault).

Model Penal Code. MPC § 211.1(2) proscribes the following as the more serious (than simple assault) crime of aggravated assault: "A person is guilty of aggravated assault if he: (a) attempts to cause serious bodily injury to another, or causes such injury purposely, knowingly or recklessly under circumstances manifesting extreme indifference to the value of human life; or (b) attempts to cause or purposely or knowingly causes bodily injury to another with a deadly weapon."

"Serious bodily injury" is defined in the MPC as "bodily injury which creates a substantial risk of death or which causes serious, permanent disfigurement, or protracted loss or impairment of the function of any bodily member or organ." MPC § 210.0(3).

Modern assault crimes. More recently still, many jurisdictions have enacted newer forms of serious aggravated assault crimes focused upon particularly heinous forms of assaultive conduct, e.g. stalking, ethnic intimidation, and cyberbullying. The elements of these sorts of crimes also vary widely jurisdiction by jurisdiction.

ASSAULT CHECKLIST

A. **Traditional Assault Crimes**—common law offenses.

1. **Battery**—intentional touching resulting in injury.

2. **Assault**—intentionally placing another in actual and reasonable fear of imminent battery.

   a. **No Touching Necessary**—includes acts intended only to scare another even if no physical contact, but verbal threats alone may not suffice.

   b. **No Real Danger Necessary**—victim's reasonable fear of battery enough.

   c. **Attempted Battery**—assault often treated as attempted battery.

   d. **Attempted Assault**—not a crime.

B. **Merger**—assault and battery elements commonly merged today into one simple assault crime.

1. **Combined Elements**—simple assault established by proof of either common law assault or battery.

2. **Simple Assault**—intentionally placing another person in fear of an imminent battery or intentionally committing a battery.

C. **Aggravated Assault**—wide variety of assault statutes punishing more severely assaults deemed to be more violent or serious.

ILLUSTRATIVE PROBLEMS

The following problems illustrate how the checklist points help to resolve questions relating to assaultive crimes.

■ PROBLEM 10.1 ■

As a practical joke, Joel Buffet hid in his roommate's, Lowell Wysor's, bedroom closet and when Wysor entered his room, Buffet burst out, wearing a mask that obscured his face. He was also holding a "gun" on Wysor, and he yelled, "Freeze, sucker!" The "gun" was not a real gun, however. It was a toy: a very realistic-looking water pistol.

Wysor, not realizing that this was all intended as a practical joke, had a heart attack and was hospitalized briefly. Is Buffet guilty of assault?

Analysis

Yes.

Buffet has intentionally placed Wysor in fear of an imminent battery. Wysor honestly and reasonably feared that he was going to be "touched" against his will, leading directly to his heart attack.

It does not matter in this analysis that Buffet did not intend that Wysor have a heart attack or that he did not otherwise intend to hurt him. Buffet is guilty of assault even though he may have intended only to scare Wysor without actually touching him at all.

Moreover, Buffet is guilty of assault even though Wysor was not really in any danger as the gun was a toy and the attack was a joke. Wysor's reasonable fear of a battery was enough to establish the commission of an assault.

■ PROBLEM 10.2 ■

Lawrence Fox, who was more than a little intoxicated, was present at his high school senior prom, dancing with his prom date, Eloise Parker. All of a sudden, for no clear reason, Fox grabbed Parker by the arm and swung her violently around the dance floor for about fifteen seconds while Parker tried unsuccessfully to resist and break free from his grip.

After finally letting her go, Parker had bright red marks on her arm where Fox had grasped it so tightly. The red marks were clearly visible on her arm for five minutes or so. Is Fox guilty of assault?

Analysis

No.

On these facts, it does not appear that Fox intentionally placed Parker in a situation where she was reasonably in fear of an imminent battery—an intentional touching against her will *that injured her as a result*—or that Fox intentionally committed such a battery. The red marks on Parker's arm would not likely be deemed sufficient in and of themselves to prove a significant enough injury to justify an assault conviction.

Had Fox's irrationally exuberant conduct resulted, of course, in more serious and painful bruising instead (or worse), the result in this case might well be different.

POINTS TO REMEMBER

- Common law battery is intentional touching resulting in injury.
- Common law assault is intentionally placing another in actual and reasonable fear of imminent battery.
- Common law assault is often treated as attempted battery.
- No physical contact or real danger is necessary to establish assault.
- Attempted assault is not a crime.

- Assault and battery elements have merged into simple assault.
- Simple assault is established by proof of either assault or battery.
- Aggravated assault statutes are more serious statutory forms of assault.

CHAPTER 11

Sex Crimes

Sex crimes are essentially assaults and/or batteries, *see* Chapter 10 (Assault), with the additional required element of proof of a specified sexual component. The applicable law defining and relating to rape and other sex crimes has changed significantly in recent years, well before the increased attention to sexual assaults engendered by the #MeToo movement starting in 2017.

Common law rape. Under the common law, the most serious sex offense—rape—was an act of sexual intercourse, including vaginal penetration however slight, committed by a male with a female not his wife, without her consent, and using force or the threat of force.

Common law evidentiary requirements. Additionally, the crime of rape was not established at common law unless:

- the victim "resisted" the attack "to the utmost";
- corroborating evidence existed in addition to the victim's own testimony;
- and the victim reported the attack to the police quickly (the so-called "fresh complaint" rule).

Moreover, evidence of the victim's lack of chastity and prior sexual conduct was admissible in rape prosecutions to impeach the victim's testimony about what had occurred.

Cumulatively, these restrictions made the crime of rape unusually difficult to prosecute. They also caused many victims to be unwilling to press charges and many prosecutors to be reluctant to file them.

Modern sex crimes. Most jurisdictions have more recently made the crime of rape less difficult to prosecute by both:

- eliminating or revising some of the common law elements of rape;

- and by eliminating or restricting the use of the common law evidentiary requirements which were unique to sexual assault cases.

In addition, in most states, "rape-shield statutes" now prevent the introduction in rape prosecutions of irrelevant evidence of a victim's past sexual conduct.

Modern rape statutes also apply expressly to sexual assaults by females as well as males.

Further, many rape statutes today apply to situations beyond the scope of the common law offense, e.g. to sexual contact with unconscious or incompetent victims, sexual contact with patients, students or others who are in an accused person's care, sexual contact induced by fraud or through the use of intoxicants, and to forcible or non-consensual anal or oral sex. Spousal rape is also a crime today, as discussed below.

Most (but not all) jurisdictions have a statute of limitations barring the prosecution of rape charges after a set period of time (often 10 or 21 years), although there has been movement toward eliminating that restriction in some states as a result of the #MeToo movement.

Moreover, also as discussed below, in addition to the crime of rape, most jurisdictions have enacted a number of less serious sex crimes with less (and less difficult to prove) elements and with concomitantly less severe penalties.

A. FORCE REQUIREMENT

One of the elements of rape at common law was the requirement that the accused engaged in sexual intercourse through the use of force or threat of force. An additional—and entirely separate—element was that the sex act occurred without the victim's consent.

Today, some jurisdictions do not require proof of *both* the use of force and the absence of consent. Instead, often rape statutes today require proof of only one of these two elements, as dictated by the particular statute reflecting legislative judgment.

In those jurisdictions where the use of force remains a required element of the crime of rape, such force or threat of force typically refers to the use of physical force. But, in some jurisdictions, it also includes the use of psychological pressure by the accused.

Threat of force. The threat of force may be verbal (e.g. "I'll kill you if you don't give me what I want") or non-verbal (e.g. a knife to the throat). It does, however, need to be a threat of death or serious physical harm to the victim or another person.

Moreover, where sexual intercourse is accomplished by means of a threat, the victim's fear of the use of force causing him or her to submit to sexual activity must be both real and reasonable for the crime of rape to be made out.

Resistance. As noted previously, at common law, a sexual assault victim needed to resist to the utmost before a rape prosecution could succeed. This requirement has been eliminated today in every jurisdiction in the United States.

However, some jurisdictions still define the requisite level of force necessary to establish forcible rape by reference to the actor's actions in overcoming a victim's reasonable resistance. As a result, a victim's resistance may still be relevant, although no longer required as a matter of law for a rape prosecution to succeed.

B. ABSENCE OF CONSENT

As previously mentioned, most jurisdictions today do not require proof of both force and the absence of consent. Instead, most rape statutes require proof only of one of those two different elements.

A common criticism of the absence of consent requirement is that, in practice, it means that the victim must prove that he or she did not consent to the sex act in question. We do not have that sort of requirement with any other criminal offense in the Crimes Code, e.g. we do not make robbery victims prove that they did not consent to the taking of their wallets.

In response to criticisms of this sort, rape statutes in many jurisdictions were amended to require proof only of the use of force, and not the absence of consent. However, even in a jurisdiction where a rape statute focuses only on an accused person's use of force, consent issues often arise in any event as—arguably—no force exists where the supposed victim has actually consented to the violent sexual activity at issue.

Good consent. The absence of consent need not be verbal (e.g. "No!"). It can be inferred from a person's actions.

For affirmative consent to sexual activity to be effective, it must be freely and voluntarily given by a competent person. It is not freely and voluntarily given, for example, when it is the product of force, deception or duress, or the victim is otherwise so impaired that he or she cannot freely consent.

Yes can turn to no. A good consent may be withdrawn at any point before sexual intercourse has actually begun. And a good consent may be withdrawn even after intercourse has begun, e.g. because the activity has become unexpectedly violent.

C. MENS REA

Traditionally, the crime of rape has been treated like a strict liability offense. *See* Chapter 3 (Mens Rea). More specifically, to establish rape in most jurisdictions, the prosecution does not need to prove that the accused knew or should have known that his victim did not consent.

Mistake. In some jurisdictions, a mistake of fact about the victim's consent, *see* Chapter 4 (Mistake), is a defense to rape. In those jurisdictions, an accused rapist can defend by proving that he honestly and reasonably believed that his victim consented to the sex act in question.

But in many jurisdictions, mistake is not a defense since the rape offense has no mens rea to which the mistaken belief would apply.

D. SPOUSAL RAPE

At common law and until relatively recently, a husband could not rape his wife as a matter of law. In large part, this immunity stemmed from the outdated and sexist belief that a wife had no grounds to refuse her husband's demands that she engage in sexual intercourse with him.

More recently, in most jurisdictions, this spousal-rape exemption has either been eliminated altogether from rape statutes, or a separate statute has been enacted creating a separate spousal rape offense. Such separate offenses are typically punished less severely than the rape of a non-spouse.

Moreover, in some of the jurisdictions with a separate statute, the spousal rape offense contains a "fresh complaint" requirement, a requirement that has been eliminated with respect to other non-spousal sexual assaults.

E. LESSER SEX OFFENSES

Most jurisdictions today criminalize a number of sex crimes in addition to the most serious crime of rape. For example, sex crimes exist today in many jurisdictions that do not require actual penetration of the victim's genitals (as the common law did). Such modern sex offenses might include instead the actus reus of the unwanted touching of another person's genitals or genital area, or of a female's breasts.

Examples. Other "lesser" sex crimes commonly criminalized include such offenses as:

- indecent exposure;
- bestiality;
- indecent assault;
- aggravated indecent assault;
- indecent contact;
- aggravated indecent contact;
- invasive visual recording (e.g. "upskirting");
- institutional sexual assault;
- and voyeurism.

F. STATUTORY RAPE

Statutory rape is sexual intercourse with a minor who is below a specified age, often called "the age of consent." Significantly, this crime is committed whether or not the minor victim has consented, and whether or not the accused has used force to commit the offense.

Accordingly, unlike the crime of rape when absence of consent is an element, the victim's consent is *not* a defense to the crime of statutory rape.

Mistake. Statutory rape is usually a strict liability crime. It does not matter whether the accused person intended to commit this crime or not. *See* Chapter 3 (Mens Rea).

As a result, an accused person's mistake about his or her victim's age ("she looked like she was over 16") is not a defense to a charge of statutory rape. *See* Chapter 4 (Mistake).

A few jurisdictions, however, do provide by statute for a defense of reasonable mistake of age where the victim is below the age of consent but nonetheless above a specified minimum age (14 perhaps). MPC § 213.6 takes this approach: "Whenever . . . the criminality of conduct depends on a child's being below the age of 10, it is no defense that the actor did not know the child's age, or reasonably believed the child to be older than 10. When criminality depends on the child's being below a critical age other than 10, it is a defense for the actor to prove by a preponderance of the evidence that he reasonably believed the child to be above the critical age."

Age gap. Statutory rape in some jurisdictions also requires proof of a specified age gap between the accused and the victim. For example, with a victim under the age of 16, in some states, the accused would have to be at least four years older before the crime of statutory rape would occur.

SEX CRIMES CHECKLIST

A. **In General**—sex crimes are assaults and/or batteries with a specified sexual element.

1. **Common Law Rape**—sexual intercourse by a male with a female not his wife, including vaginal penetration however slight, without consent and using force or threat of force.

2. **Common Law Evidentiary Requirements**—restrictions made rape difficult to prosecute and many victims and prosecutors unwilling to press charges.

    a. **Resistance**—victim needed to resist attack "to the utmost."

    b. **Corroboration**—corroborating evidence needed beyond victim's testimony.

    c. **Fresh Complaint**—victim needed to report attack quickly.

    d. **Impeachment**—evidence of victim's prior sexual conduct admissible to impeach victim's testimony.

3. **Modern Sex Crimes**—rape less difficult to prosecute today.

    a. **Changes from Common Law**

        i. **Elements**—common law elements eliminated or revised.

        ii. **Evidence**—requirements unique to rape cases eliminated or restricted.

        iii. **Rape-Shield Laws**—prevent introduction of irrelevant evidence of past sexual conduct.

        iv. **Gender Neutral**—apply to females as well as males.

    b. **Crimes Beyond Rape**—sexual assaults less serious than rape also criminalized.

c. **Statute of Limitations**—rape prosecution barred after period of years but some movement to end such restrictions.

B. **Force**—common law element of rape.

1. **Modern Change**—often rape statutes today require force or absence of consent, not both.

2. **Beyond Physical**—sometimes includes use of psychological pressure by accused as well as physical.

3. **Threat of Force**—may be verbal or non-verbal.

a. **Serious Threats Only**—must be threat of death or serious physical harm to victim or another person.

b. **Reasonable Fear**—victim's fear of force must be real and reasonable.

4. **Resistance**—victim no longer needs to resist but some jurisdictions define force by reference to overcoming victim's reasonable resistance.

C. **Absence of Consent**—common law element of rape.

1. **Modern Change**—often rape statutes today require force or absence of consent, not both.

2. **Good Consent**—must be freely and voluntarily given by competent person.

a. **Lack of Consent Need Not Be Verbal**—absence of consent can be inferred from actions.

b. **Not Coerced**—cannot be product of force, deception or duress.

c. **Not Impaired**—impaired victim not capable of good consent.

d. **Yes Can Change to No**—good consent may be withdrawn before or after intercourse has begun.

D. **Mens Rea**—traditionally treated like strict liability.

1. **Knowledge of Consent**—no need to prove accused knew or should have known that victim did not consent.

2. **Mistake**—in many jurisdictions, no defense that accused honestly and reasonably believed victim consented.

E. **Spousal Rape**—not a crime at common law.

1. **Modern Change**—common law abrogated.

a. **Immunity Eliminated**—same as rape in some states.

b. **Separate Crime**—separate spousal rape crime in some states, less serious than rape and fresh complaint requirement.

F. **Lesser Offenses**—more sex crimes than just rape today with less serious elements and punishments.

G. **Statutory Rape**—sexual intercourse with a minor below age of consent whether or not good consent or use of force.

1. **Mistake About Age Not a Defense**—minority permit defense of reasonable mistake of age within specified age range.

2. **Age Gap**—some jurisdictions require proof of specified age gap between accused and victim.

ILLUSTRATIVE PROBLEMS

The following problems illustrate how the checklist points help to resolve questions relating to sex crimes.

■ PROBLEM 11.1 ■

John Patterson and Sarah Donohue, both college sophomores, met at a fraternity party and ended the evening back in Donohue's single dormitory room. After talking and flirting and drinking wine for a half hour or so, they began kissing and hugging each other. Eventually, Patterson started to remove Donohue's clothing, but she stopped him, saying: "No. No. Not now. Maybe later." Hearing that, Patterson stopped his efforts to take Donohue's clothes off. They talked and kissed some more, and eventually both of them fell asleep in the dorm room.

In the middle of the night, Patterson woke up and saw that Donohue was sleeping right next to him. He then reached over, pulled her skirt and underwear off, and had sexual intercourse with her. Prior to and during this sex act, Donohue said nothing at all. Her eyes were shut. She appeared to still be asleep or unconscious. But after Patterson rolled off of her, Donohue roused herself and yelled at him: "Why did you do that? I told you no!" Patterson responded: "You said 'later.' It was later. I thought you wanted me to do that. Hey, you didn't complain!"

Donohue threw Patterson out of her room and called the campus police who promptly arrested him. Is Patterson guilty of rape?

Analysis

Probably.

Under the common law, and in a jurisdiction that defines rape by using an absence-of-consent element but not a use-of-force element, this is clearly rape. Simply put, Donohue said "no." No means no. She did not freely and voluntarily consent to sexual intercourse with Patterson. This is a classic "date rape" scenario.

But, in a jurisdiction that defines rape by using a use-of-force element but not an absence-of-consent element, it is less clear whether or not this is rape. The fact that Donohue did not resist Patterson is irrelevant. Resistance is no longer required as a matter of law as it was at common law. The question would be whether Patterson accomplished this sex act by use of force, the sort of force perhaps which would overcome the resistance of a reasonable person.

If Donohue was really asleep when all of this occurred (or in an alcoholic stupor perhaps and unconscious)—a fact question for the jury—then this conduct is clearly rape as the act of intercourse was accomplished entirely by Patterson's acts of forcibly removing Donohue's clothes and penetrating her when she was unable to acquiesce (and perhaps impaired if she was intoxicated at the time).

If Donohue was actually awake during the sex act, however, and not consenting but simply acquiescing—another fact question—Patterson's conduct would not be rape. That is, assuming once again that this occurred in a jurisdiction where absence-of-consent is not an element of rape.

Parenthetically, even in the latter scenario, even if these facts did not constitute rape due to the arguable absence of force, these facts would very likely establish commission of a different sex crime, albeit a crime less serious than rape, e.g. indecent contact or aggravated indecent contact.

■ PROBLEM 11.2 ■

Gordon Lewis approached Susan Staples, who was out walking her dog in a dark and deserted part of town late one night, and asked her to have sex with him. Staples didn't respond to Lewis. Instead, she just turned right around and started running away from him. Lewis ran after her. He caught up to her, grabbed her by the arm, and threw her to the ground. "You know what I want," he said, "and if you don't give it to me that mutt of yours is dead meat." Rather than risk harm to her dog, Staples submitted to Lewis's demands and had sexual intercourse with him.

Was Lewis guilty of rape?

Analysis

It is likely, but it nonetheless depends.

Under the common law, and in a jurisdiction that defines rape by using an absence-of-consent element but not a use-of-force element, this is clearly rape. There is no question but that Staples did not freely and voluntarily consent to sexual intercourse with Lewis.

But, in a jurisdiction that defines rape by using a use-of-force element but not an absence-of-consent element, it is less clear whether or not this is rape. The fact that Staples did not resist Lewis is irrelevant. Resistance is no longer required as a matter of law as it was at common law. The question would be whether Lewis accomplished this sex act by use of force, the sort of force perhaps which would overcome the resistance of a reasonable person. If this is a jurisdiction that permits the use of psychological force to establish the force element of rape, then this conduct is clearly a sufficient threat as the act of intercourse was accomplished entirely as a result of Lewis's psychological coercion.

But was Staples' fear sufficient as a matter of law? Perhaps not, as her primary concern was physical harm to her dog and not to herself or to another person. On the other hand, it would be hard to believe that Staples was not equally concerned about her own well-being in these circumstances. If she testified as much, the likelihood of a rape conviction on these facts would increase substantially.

Parenthetically, whether or not this conduct would constitute rape in the jurisdiction in which it occurred, it might well suffice to establish commission of a different sex crime, albeit a crime less serious than rape, e.g. indecent contact or aggravated indecent contact.

Moreover, on these facts, even if this activity did not constitute rape, it might well be the separate crime of attempted rape. *See* Chapter 7 (Attempt).

■ PROBLEM 11.3 ■

Stuart Hancock met Lisa Little at an amusement park and one thing led to another and they ended up having sexual intercourse later that evening in the backseat of Hancock's car. After the fact, however, Little claimed that she hadn't meant for things to go that far and that she had not agreed to having intercourse. Hancock was shocked because he thought that her lack of any verbal response to his actions and behavior indicated her interest in and agreement to having sex with him.

Hancock is nineteen years old. Little is only thirteen years old, but she told Hancock that she was seventeen. Moreover, in terms of physical maturity, Little looked to be at least seventeen years old at the time these events occurred.

Is Hancock guilty of either rape or statutory rape?

Analysis

Depending on the applicable statutes, Hancock may be guilty of both crimes.

Under the common law, and in a jurisdiction that defines rape by using an absence-of-consent element but not a use-of-force element, this is clearly rape. If Little's claim of non-acquiescence is deemed credible by the jury, she did not freely and voluntarily consent to sexual intercourse with Hancock. It does not matter that Hancock may have believed that she did. Nor does it matter that his belief may have been reasonable. In a majority of jurisdictions, it is no defense that a person accused of rape honestly and reasonably believed that his victim consented to have intercourse.

But, in a jurisdiction that defines rape by using a use-of-force element but not an absence-of-consent element, it is less clear whether or not this is rape. The fact that Little did not resist Hancock is irrelevant. Resistance is no longer required as a matter of law as it was at common law. The question would be whether Hancock accomplished this act of sexual intercourse by use of force, the sort of force perhaps which would overcome the resistance of a reasonable person. On these facts, it would not appear that this degree of force was present (although this is a factual question for the jury).

Whether or not this conduct constitutes rape, it is, however, clearly statutory rape. That is, assuming (as is likely) that the age of consent in this jurisdiction is older than thirteen years, and assuming that the statutory rape statute does not contain (as is also likely) an age gap exclusion of six years or more.

Hancock's conduct is statutory rape whether or not Little is found to have consented to the sexual intercourse as the absence of consent is not an element of statutory rape.

Moreover, in a majority of jurisdictions, even an honest and reasonable mistake as to a sex partner's age is not a good defense. Hence, Hancock's reasonable belief that Little was seventeen is irrelevant.

POINTS TO REMEMBER

- Rape statutes today typically require proof of force or absence of consent, not both.
- Most common law evidentiary restrictions that made prosecution of rape case unusually difficult have been eliminated.
- Rape-shield laws restrict introduction of irrelevant evidence of a victim's past sexual conduct.
- Sex crimes less serious than rape are also criminalized.
- A force element is satisfied by psychological as well as physical force in some jurisdictions.
- Threat of force may be verbal or non-verbal.
- Threat of force must be threat of death or serious physical harm.
- Threat of force must create actual and reasonable fear in victim.
- Victims no longer need to resist but force may be defined as sufficient to overcome reasonable resistance.
- Consent to sex must be freely and voluntarily given.
- Absence of consent to sex does not need to be verbal.
- Victim may change mind about consent before or after intercourse begins.
- It is no defense that accused reasonably believed victim consented.
- Spousal rape is a crime.
- Consent is irrelevant in statutory rape cases.
- Mistake as to age is irrelevant in statutory rape cases.

CHAPTER 12

Homicide

Modern homicide crimes. Today, a number of different crimes involving killing—homicide crimes—exist in every jurisdiction. These range from the homicide offense that the legislature has deemed to be the most heinous type of killing to the homicide offense deemed least heinous, with a corresponding difference in potential sentence upon conviction.

Homicide by degrees. In many jurisdictions, homicide offenses today—particularly the crime of murder—are distinguished from one another by reference to "degrees," with the highest degree being the most heinous of the crimes, e.g. first-degree murder, second-degree murder, etc.

Homicide elements. All homicide crimes require proof of a killing act committed by the accused which caused the death of a human being. *See* Chapter 2 (Actus Reus) & Chapter 5 (Causation).

The primary and most significant distinction between the various homicide offenses in every jurisdiction is the different mens rea required to establish each one. See Chapter 3 (Mens Rea). Typically, the more difficult the mens rea is to prove, the more serious the homicide offense.

Some homicide offenses are intentional killings and some are unintentional killings. The latter are generally viewed as less heinous and are, accordingly, punished less severely. Intentional killings are usually seen and punished as the worst kinds of homicides.

Corpus delicti rule. A common law rule of evidence used in most jurisdictions, the corpus delicti rule, prohibits the admission of an accused person's confession at a criminal trial until the prosecution first introduces independent evidence that the crime described in the confession actually occurred.

Common law. Murder and manslaughter are homicide crimes with common law roots. Killing another human being with "malice aforethought" (also called "malice prepense") was murder. Killing another human being without "malice aforethought" was manslaughter.

At common law, and in a majority of jurisdictions, a fetus—even a viable fetus—is not a human being for these purposes.

A. MURDER

1. First Degree: Premeditation & Deliberation

Premeditated murder, often called murder in the first degree, is an intentional killing undertaken with malice that is also premeditated, willful and deliberate.

First degree or premeditated murder is the most serious homicide crime. In some jurisdictions, a conviction for first degree murder can be punished by capital punishment. *See* Chapter 1 (Nature of Criminal Law).

Malice aforethought. Malice aforethought (or "malice prepense"), taken from the common law, refers to a particularly heinous ill will on the part of a killer. Malice was traditionally described as wickedness of disposition, hardness of heart, wanton conduct, cruelty, recklessness of consequences, and/or a mind without regard to social duty.

Malice was the distinguishing factor between murder and manslaughter at common law, and remains so in most jurisdictions, although today it is largely a legal term of art which can be proven in a variety of different ways.

Express or implied. Where malice is a required element of proof, it may be established by the prosecution proving expressly that the accused had the specific intent to kill the victim, or it may be (and often is) simply inferred from the attendant circumstances.

In many jurisdictions, malice can be implied from an accused person's killing act committed with gross recklessness and/or from the accused person's actions which demonstrate extreme indifference to the value of human life. In addition, malice is often inferred where a person has killed another person by using a deadly weapon (e.g. a gun or a knife) on a vital part of the victim's body.

Premeditation and deliberation. A conviction for premeditated murder also requires proof of actual, prior thought and reflection by the accused about the killing act in question.

Jurisdictions vary significantly, however, on the question how substantial such reflection must be in order to establish this premeditation and deliberation element. Some states require a showing of sustained and meaningful deliberation to make out this element; other states require only a demonstration of momentary reflection.

No time is too short. A majority of states take the latter—momentary reflection—approach. In those states, it is often said that "no time is too short"—even a few seconds—for a killer to actually premeditate and deliberate about a killing sufficiently to justify a conviction for first degree murder.

The amount of time of reflection, however, is not the only factor that juries may and do take into account in determining whether premeditation and deliberation exist. Juries may also consider, for example, evidence of:

- any prior planning activity on the accused person's part;
- the accused person's prior relationship with the victim;
- any motive that the accused may have had for the killing;
- and the manner of the killing itself, i.e. did it reflect some sort of preconceived design?

2. Second Degree: Malice Aforethought Without Premeditation & Deliberation

Second-degree murder is usually defined as a killing undertaken with malice, but without the premeditation and deliberation necessary to establish first degree murder. Sometimes such killings are called "impulse killings" to distinguish them from premeditated killings.

Model Penal Code: depraved heart murder. Model Penal Code (MPC) § 210.2(1)(b) provides in relevant part that "criminal homicide constitutes murder when. . . it is committed recklessly under circumstances manifesting extreme indifference to the value of human life." The MPC calls this type of homicide "depraved heart murder."

3. Felony Murder

Common law. At common law, a death that occurred while an accused person was committing or attempting to commit a felony was also deemed to be murder. This is felony murder.

Model Penal Code. The MPC presumes reckless indifference when a killing occurs during the commission of a specified list of felonies, reaching essentially the same result as the felony murder rule. MPC § 210.2(1)(b) provides in relevant part that "criminal homicide constitutes murder when. . . it is committed recklessly under circumstances manifesting extreme indifference to the value of human life. Such recklessness and indifference are presumed if the actor is engaged or is an accomplice in the commission of, or an attempt to commit, or flight after committing or attempting to commit robbery, rape or deviate sexual intercourse by force or threat of force, arson, burglary, kidnapping or felonious escape."

Modern rule. In a majority of jurisdictions today, felony murder is either viewed as one way to establish murder (by imputing malice through transferred intent from the accused person's commission of a felonious act), or it is simply treated as a separate homicide offense.

To establish felony murder, the prosecution must prove all of the elements of a specified triggering felony and, in addition, that someone died in the process. Common triggering felonies for felony murder include commission of or an attempt to commit:

- robbery;
- rape;
- arson;
- burglary;
- kidnapping;
- carjacking;
- and terrorism.

In some jurisdictions, however, instead of a list of applicable triggering felonies, the felony murder rule applies instead to any felony deemed to be inherently dangerous to human life during the commission of which someone died.

Independent felony. The triggering felony for a felony murder prosecution must be independent of or collateral to the acts leading to the victim's death.

When the underlying felony is an integral part of the victim's death—an aggravated assault, for example, *see* Chapter 10 (Assault)—and the accused had no independent felonious purpose—as he or she would have with a sexual assault, for example, *see* Chapter 11 (Sex Crimes)—the felony murder rule is inapplicable. It "merges" with the homicide. Some other type of homicide crime may exist on such facts, but this is not a felony murder.

Acts of accomplices and others. In some states, an accused person is not deemed necessarily responsible for a killing act that takes place during the course of a felony if it was committed by an accomplice. *See* Chapter 6 (Accomplice & Vicarious Liability).

Instead, a defense is available to the non-killing felon. This defense applies, however, only where the accused did not know or foresee that his or her accomplice would kill in the course of the felony and where he or she was neither armed with a deadly weapon nor knew that any of his or her accomplices was so armed.

In a majority of jurisdictions, a felon is not usually held to be responsible for the unforeseeable killing acts of someone other than an accomplice that occurred during the course of the felony. A killing that occurs when a third person responds with deadly force to the accused person's or the accused person's accomplices' provocative acts (often gunfire) would be foreseeable, and the accused may be held responsible for such a killing act. This includes the killing of the accused person's accomplice and co-felon.

Res gestae requirement. To meet the felony murder requirement that the death occurred during the commission of a felony, the death must satisfy the res gestae requirement. This means that there must be temporal and physical proximity (close in time and place) between the death and the felony, and that the death was causally related to the accused person's felonious acts. *See* Chapter 5 (Causation).

Flight after felony. The felony murder doctrine also applies to deaths that occur as a person is escaping after the commission of a felony. Although there is some dispute about the appropriate test to use to determine when such flight has ended, many courts use the test of asking whether the felon has reached a point of "safe haven." At that point, the felony murder doctrine no longer applies.

B. MANSLAUGHTER

1. Voluntary Manslaughter

Mitigated murder. Voluntary manslaughter is an intentional killing that has been mitigated from murder, usually because the accused killer was found to have been reasonably provoked and therefore lacked the malice necessary to establish murder.

Mitigating defense. Because voluntary manslaughter is mitigated murder, criminal defendants often attempt to use it as a partial defense to a murder charge, i.e. an accused person charged with murder defends by trying to convince a jury that he or she committed voluntary manslaughter instead. Of course, unlike a complete defense (a defense that would excuse the accused from all criminal charges), if an accused successfully makes such a mitigating defense, he or she is still convicted of a crime, voluntary manslaughter in this case.

A defendant can try and make both a complete and a mitigating defense at the same time, e.g. "I killed her, but I was insane" (a complete defense, *see* Chapter 15 (Excuses)), "but even if you think that I was sane, I was reasonably provoked" and the homicide was only voluntary manslaughter (a mitigating defense).

a. Provocation Defense: Heat of Passion

Murder is mitigated to voluntary manslaughter where an accused person can establish that he or she killed in the "heat of passion." This passion (sometimes referred to as "seeing red") negatives the malice element required to establish murder.

The provocation defense is not available to mitigate murder to manslaughter, however, where the accused has had a reasonable "cooling-off period" to recover from his or her impassioned condition.

Voluntary manslaughter is established when the accused is found to have acted pursuant to a sudden and intense passion resulting from a provocation by the victim so serious that it would create such a passion in a reasonable person. Voluntary manslaughter also applies where an impassioned accused kills someone other than the person who provoked him or her in an attempt to kill the provoker.

i. Adequate Provocative Acts

Under the common law, only a handful of provocative acts were considered adequate to mitigate murder to voluntary manslaughter. These included:

- a physical attack;
- observation of adultery of a spouse;
- being put in fear;
- an illegal arrest;
- and an assault on a close relative.

Today, however, in most jurisdictions, almost any act can be considered adequately provocative to support a provocation defense if the jury finds that a reasonable person would have been so provoked. In assessing whether a "reasonable person" would have been provoked, jurors are often instructed to put themselves "in the shoes" of the defendant. However, jurors may not consider extraordinary characteristics of the defendant, such as his or her "hot temper," lack of self control, or pathological behavior, for example.

ii. Words: Sticks & Stones Doctrine

At common law, mere words alone could never be deemed an adequate provocation to mitigate murder to voluntary manslaughter. This has sometimes been called the "sticks and stones doctrine" because of the classic children's chant: "Sticks and stones can break my bones, but words can never hurt me." The theory is that reasonable people should be able to resist becoming impassioned by words alone.

Many jurisdictions today reject this doctrine, however, recognizing the possibility that a reasonable person could in fact be provoked by particularly hurtful words.

In any event, provocative words are quite often accompanied by provocative actions which can—taken together—be an adequate source of provocation in any jurisdiction.

b. Imperfect Defense

In many jurisdictions, in addition to the provocation defense described above, voluntary manslaughter can also be established by means of the use of an "imperfect defense."

An imperfect defense is a traditional protective defense like self defense or defense of others, *see* Chapter 14 (Justification Defense), where an accused person honestly believed that he or she needed to kill in order to take justified protective action, but that belief of the accused was unreasonable.

2. Involuntary Manslaughter

Involuntary manslaughter is an unintentional killing that is committed without malice.

The mens rea showing required for involuntary manslaughter varies significantly by jurisdiction. In many jurisdictions, the mens rea required is "gross negligence" (sometimes called "criminal negligence"). *See* Chapter 3 (Mens Rea). This is in contrast to "ordinary negligence" (sometimes called "civil negligence") which is the mental state necessary to make out the tort of negligence. A greater showing is required to establish gross (criminal) rather than ordinary (civil) negligence.

MPC § 210.3(1)(a)—and some jurisdictions as well—require the higher showing of recklessness to establish the mens rea of involuntary manslaughter. This is a significant difference between the definition of this offense in different jurisdictions as recklessness requires proof that the accused "consciously" disregarded a risk of death while a showing of criminal negligence does not. *See* Chapter 3 (Mens Rea).

In stark contrast, a very few jurisdictions provide that an involuntary manslaughter conviction can be based upon a lower showing of ordinary (tort) rather than criminal or gross negligence.

3. Misdemeanor Manslaughter

At common law, a misdemeanor manslaughter rule made it manslaughter for a person to commit a misdemeanor, during the occurrence of which a death occurred. This rule was rejected by the MPC, and has been abolished in most states.

C. NEGLIGENT & VEHICULAR HOMICIDE

1. Negligent Homicide

MPC § 210.4—and some jurisdictions—criminalize the separate offense of negligent homicide. In a jurisdiction where involuntary manslaughter requires proof of recklessness (rather than criminal negligence), the separate crime of negligent homicide creates a lesser level of homicide which applies to those killings that occur merely as a result of an accused person's criminal negligence.

2. Vehicular Homicide

A number of jurisdictions have enacted homicide crimes that apply strictly to deaths that occurred while an accused person was driving a car and violating an applicable traffic law. Depending on the jurisdiction, such crimes might have either a recklessness or (civil or criminal) negligence mens rea.

Sometimes, other than the requisite element of violation of a traffic law, these statutes overlap with the crime of involuntary manslaughter. But the fact that a person was driving a car when he or she killed someone should not and does not mean, however, that he or she must be prosecuted under a vehicular homicide statute. In the appropriate circumstances, any homicide crime—even first degree murder—might apply to the killing act of the driver of a vehicle.

HOMICIDE CHECKLIST

A. **In General**—specific homicide crimes vary widely by jurisdiction.

1. **Common Law**—murder and manslaughter.

    a. **Murder**—killing another human being with "malice aforethought."

    b. **Manslaughter**—killing another human being without "malice aforethought."

    c. **Human Being**—not a fetus.

2. **Modern Homicide Crimes**—number of crimes, often separated by degrees.

3. **Elements**—killing act causing death of human being and specified mens rea.

B. **Murder**—need malice, express or implied.

1. **Malice Aforethought**—traditionally, wickedness of disposition, hardness of heart, wanton conduct, cruelty, recklessness of consequences, a mind without regard to social duty; legal term of art today.

    a. **Express**—proof of malicious thoughts or activity.

    b. **Implied**—implied from gross recklessness or extreme indifference to value of human life.

    c. **Presumption**—often presumed where use of deadly weapon on vital part of victim's body.

2. **First Degree**—also need premeditation and deliberation (p & d).

    a. **Intentional Killing**—specific intent to kill.

    b. **P & D**—actual prior thought and reflection.

        i. **Time**—key element.

            A. **Majority**—no time is too short.

            B. **Minority**—must be meaningful deliberation.

        ii. **Other Factors**—prior planning activity; prior relationship with victim; motive; and manner of killing.

3. **Second Degree**—malice without p & d.

4. **Felony Murder**—death occurring during felony or attempted felony.

   a. **Triggering Felony**—must prove all elements of specified felony.

      i. **Common List**—majority: list including robbery, rape, arson, burglary, and kidnapping.

      ii. **Dangerous Felonies**—minority: any dangerous felony.

      iii. **Independent Felony**—triggering felony must be independent of acts leading to victim's death.

      iv. **Res Gestae**—death must occur in proximity to and be caused by accused's acts.

   b. **Killing by Accomplices**—some states: defense that unforeseeable killing by co-felon if accused not armed with deadly weapon.

   c. **Killing by Others**—majority: not responsible for unforeseeable killing acts of others during felony.

   d. **Responsive Killing**—responsible for death, including co-felon, resulting from response to accused's or accomplices' provocative acts.

   e. **Flight After Felony**—still felony murder until felon has reached safe haven.

C. **Manslaughter**—killing without malice.

1. **Voluntary Manslaughter**—mitigated murder.

   a. **Provocation Defense**—murder in the heat of passion.

      i. **Elements**—sudden, intense passion resulting from provocation by victim so serious it would create passion in reasonable person.

      ii. **Cooling-Off Period**—no defense where reasonable "cooling-off period."

      iii. **Adequate Provocation**—common law: limited number of provocative acts; today, almost any act that would provoke reasonable person.

      iv. **Reasonable Person**—consider circumstances as if in shoes of the defendant, but not extraordinary characteristics like hot temper.

v. **Words**—common law: words alone not enough to provoke; today: can be enough.

vi. **Wrong Victim**—defense applies where killing of someone else in attempt to kill provoker.

b. **Imperfect Defense**—traditional protective defense where belief in need to kill honest but unreasonable.

2. **Involuntary Manslaughter**—unintentional killing committed without malice.

a. **Mens Rea**—varies.

i. **Majority**—gross (criminal) negligence.

ii. **Minority**—recklessness or ordinary (civil) negligence.

3. **Misdemeanor Manslaughter**—largely abandoned.

D. **Negligent Homicide**—some states: separate negligence crime where involuntary manslaughter requires recklessness.

E. **Vehicular Homicide**—killing while accused driving and violating traffic law.

1. **Mens Rea**—varies: recklessness or negligence.

2. **Not Exclusive**—any homicide crime can apply to driver of vehicle.

ILLUSTRATIVE PROBLEMS

The following problems illustrate how the checklist points help to resolve questions relating to homicide.

■ PROBLEM 12.1 ■

Walter and Darla Harris, husband and wife, had a loud and violent argument with one another in the living room of their home. Walter accused Darla of being unfaithful to him and having had sexual relations with a number of other men and women. Darla accused Walter of being dismissive, distant, and completely inattentive to her and her needs. They each pushed and shoved one other, and each of them made threats of violence against the other one. After forty-five minutes of this, Walter, seething, stomped into the bedroom, took his pistol from his dresser drawer, and returned to the living room.

Darla, seeing the gun in Walter's hand, said to him: "Think you're a big shot, huh? You don't even have the guts to shoot me, you idiot!" On that score, Darla was wrong. Dead wrong. After yelling back at Darla for another few minutes, Walter then aimed his gun directly at her head and fired once, killing her instantly.

Is Walter guilty of homicide in the shooting of Darla? If so, what homicide offense has he committed?

Analysis

Yes, Walter is definitely guilty of homicide.

As to what particular homicide offense he has committed, the answer to this question depends on the specific homicide crimes in the crimes code this jurisdiction, and on what the jury finds actually occurred.

First of all, Walter clearly committed a killing act—shooting at Darla—which caused the death of Darla, a human being. Accordingly, the only remaining question is whether the appropriate mens rea existed to establish a homicide offense.

Was this murder? Walter clearly acted maliciously. Malice could be found expressly from his shooting of Darla with recklessness as to the consequences. Indeed, malice is often presumed where a person has killed another person by using a deadly weapon on a vital part of his or her body, which is exactly what occurred here.

Moreover, even if malice was not express here, it would certainly be implied from Walter's gross recklessness in the use of the gun and from his actions demonstrating extreme indifference to the value of Darla's life. The existence of malice alone is enough to establish second degree murder (ignoring for a moment the potential provocation defense, as discussed below).

So, second degree murder is clear. But could this have been first degree murder? Yes, absolutely. It could have been.

The question is whether or not there was premeditation and deliberation here or, instead, whether this was simply an impulse killing (which would make it second degree murder)? In a jurisdiction where no time is too short to support a finding of premeditation and deliberation, there was certainly enough time for Walter to think about what he wanted to do to Darla during the pendency of the argument, when he went into the bedroom to get the gun, and even afterwards when he had returned to the living room with the gun but did not shoot right away.

Indeed, even in a jurisdiction where more time for actual reflection is required to support a finding of premeditation and deliberation, the amount of time involved here, and Walter's obvious prior (spousal) relationship with the victim, his motive (whether simple jealousy or anger at his wife), the possible indication of prior planning activity evidenced by the ready availability of the pistol, all of these factors make it quite likely that a jury would find that sufficient premeditation and deliberation existed—in any jurisdiction—to support a conviction of first degree murder.

But what of voluntary manslaughter? Walter might well argue here that he was entitled to a mitigating provocation defense, i.e. that Darla's comments and actions (including his belief in her acts of adultery) made him "see red" and, impassioned when he acted, entitled him to a verdict of voluntary manslaughter instead of murder. But Walter would have trouble meeting all of the elements of a mitigating provocation defense here.

Murder is mitigated to voluntary manslaughter only where an accused person can establish that he or she killed in the "heat of passion." It is not available where the person claiming to be so impassioned has had a reasonable "cooling-off period." Here, there is a good argument to be made that two such reasonable cooling-off periods existed; one, when Walter left the argument to enter the bedroom and find his gun; and, two, when Walter paused after Darla belittled him when he had returned with his gun to the living room and did not fire right away. It is possible that a trial judge might find as a matter of law that such a cooling-off period existed, making a defense of provocation unavailing for Walter. Moreover, for much the same reason, Walter may well not be able to establish that he acted (as he must to make out this provocation defense) "suddenly."

Additionally, it is not clear that Walter could convince a fact-finder (again, as he must) that the passion he claims to have honestly felt was so serious that it would have created just such a homicidal passion in a reasonable person. Indeed, under the common law, the provocation he claims would likely fail on grounds of adequacy.

Finding one's spouse engaging in an act of adultery was a classically adequate provocation at common law, but that is not what happened here. There is no evidence that he saw Darla do anything wrong, adultery or otherwise. He simply *thought* that she was unfaithful. Or maybe someone else told him that. Or maybe Darla told him that, taunting him. In any event, Walter was apparently responding to words—just words—and, at common law, words alone were not enough to establish provocation.

Even today, in a jurisdiction where words alone might be enough to mitigate to voluntary manslaughter, the jury would have to find that a reasonable person would have become similarly impassioned by these particular words. Such a finding is possible, of course, but it is far from certain or even likely.

As a result, for all of these reasons, it is unlikely that Walter could defend successfully with a provocation defense and mitigate this crime to voluntary manslaughter. He is most likely guilty of first degree murder, and clearly guilty of second degree murder.

Parenthetically, if the facts were changed slightly, if, for example, Walter claimed that he did not intend to shoot Darla, that his finger slipped on the trigger, and that is why he shot her—and, hypothesizing further, assuming that the jury believed this—Walter would still be guilty of homicide. In this event, he would likely be found to be—at the very least—grossly negligent in his use of a deadly weapon. Hence, he would be guilty of involuntary manslaughter or, depending on the jurisdiction's crimes code, negligent homicide if that crime was on the books.

■ PROBLEM 12.2 ■

Don Bass, Wendy Newlon and Mark Horner robbed a liquor store, holding the owner, Dulles Lambert, and two customers at gunpoint. Each of the robbers was armed and each participated in taking money out of the cash register and from the store owner and customers.

As the three robbers left the store, Lambert retrieved his sawed-off shotgun from under the counter and raced to the door to shoot at them. One of the robbers, Bass, looking back as the three made their getaway, saw Lambert aim the rifle at them and quickly took a shot at Lambert, missing him, but splintering the doorway above his head. Lambert threw himself to the ground upon hearing the gunshot and the splintering doorway and, in the process, hit his head on a loose piece of pavement as he fell, cracking his skull and killing him.

Are Bass, Newlon, and Horner guilty of homicide in the death of Lambert? If so, of what homicide offense are they guilty?

Analysis

Yes. All three are likely to be found guilty of—at the very least—felony murder.

Bass clearly committed a killing act—shooting at Lambert—which caused the death of Lambert, a human being. (For discussion of the causation issues involved in this problem, *see* Chapter 5 (Causation)).

Moreover, assuming that these events took place in a jurisdiction—the majority—that has a felony murder homicide crime in the crimes code, all that the prosecution would have to establish here to make out this offense is that Bass, Newlon, and Horner committed a triggering felony and that someone died in the course of that felony or flight afterwards.

All of those elements are present here. The felony of robbery is established clearly on these facts. *See* Chapter 13 (Theft). In a jurisdiction with a specified list of triggering felonies for felony murder, robbery is invariably included as one of those felonies. Moreover, in a jurisdiction requiring instead that a triggering felony be one that is simply inherently dangerous to human life, armed robbery clearly fills the bill.

In addition, although the death of Lambert did not occur during the commission of the felony itself, it did occur during the robbers' flight after the felony occurred and before they had reached a place of safety. Hence, the felony murder rule continues to apply.

Newlon and Horner might argue, however, that they should not be held responsible for the killing acts of their accomplice and co-felon, Bass. But this argument will not succeed. Newlon and Horner are not entitled to a defense of this sort—even if it exists in this jurisdiction—as they both were armed with deadly weapons and they both knew that Bass was armed as well. Newlon and Horner could and should have reasonably foreseen that death or serious injury might occur during this felony and, accordingly, they cannot defend by trying to disassociate themselves from their accomplice who committed the actual killing act.

But what if these events took place in a minority jurisdiction that does not have a felony murder statute? In that case, Bass, Newlon and Horner would still likely be guilty of homicide. All of the basic elements of homicide other than mental state are satisfied, as discussed previously, so the question would be what if any homicidal mens rea could be established in these circumstances for these robbers? (For a full discussion of accomplice liability principles, *see* Chapter 6 (Accomplice & Vicarious Liability).)

It is not likely that premeditation and deliberation sufficient to establish first degree murder could be found on these facts as there is insufficient evidence (arguably) of Bass's specific intent to kill Lambert. But there is every reason to believe that Bass (and his accomplices, Newlon and Horner) could be found to have acted maliciously, both expressly and impliedly, in using handguns to rob a retail establishment and in Bass's act of firing his gun at Lambert, even though he missed. As a result, even in a jurisdiction that does not possess a felony murder statute, Bass, Newlon, and Horner are likely guilty of second degree murder.

■ PROBLEM 12.3 ■

Oliver and Maria Clemente were unloading groceries from the trunk of their car when Sonny Jackson came up to them, put a knife to Oliver's back, and told Oliver to give him his wallet if he didn't want to be hurt. Jackson also told Maria to toss him her purse if she didn't want him to stab Oliver. Maria complied immediately, tossing her purse toward Jackson. But Oliver, only pretending to reach for the wallet in his back pocket, instead swung at Jackson, who, in response, stabbed Oliver seven times in the chest, resulting in his death.

Is Jackson guilty of first degree murder?

Analysis

Maybe.

First of all, Jackson clearly committed a killing act—stabbing Oliver repeatedly—which caused the death of Oliver, a human being. Accordingly, the only remaining question is whether the appropriate mens rea existed to establish first degree murder.

To establish first degree murder, the prosecution must establish the existence of malice and premeditation and deliberation. Malice is easy to find on these facts. It could be found expressly from Jackson's act of stabbing Oliver seven times with apparent recklessness of the consequences. Moreover, malice is often presumed where a person has killed another person by using a deadly weapon on a vital part of his or her body, which is exactly what occurred here. Indeed, even if malice was not express here, it would certainly be implied from Jackson's gross recklessness in the use of the knife and from his actions which clearly demonstrated extreme indifference to the value of Oliver's life.

But establishing malice is enough to prove second degree murder, not first degree murder. To prove first degree murder, in addition to malice, premeditation and deliberation must be established.

In a jurisdiction where a significant period of actual reflection is required to support a finding of premeditation and deliberation, the amount of time involved here—the instant when Oliver swung at Jackson—would likely not prove to be enough time in and of itself to support a finding of first degree murder. In contrast, in a jurisdiction where no time is too short for a person to premeditate a killing, Jackson might well be viewed as having had enough time to develop the specific intent to kill after Oliver swung at him, even though the time period may not have been more than a second or two, at most.

There is, moreover, at least one other factor present other than time that might well support a fact-finder's conclusion that premeditation and deliberation existed no matter which test this jurisdiction uses relating to the amount of time. That additional factor is the indication of prior planning activity that was evidenced by the presence of the knife used by Jackson in the attempted robbery.

In short, depending on the jurisdiction and the jury's fact-finding, there may or may not be enough evidence here to support a conviction for first degree murder here directly.

But there is one other significant possibility.

In some jurisdictions, felony murder is an indirect way to establish first degree murder, essentially by implying malice and premeditation and deliberation from the felonious intent. If the events in this problem took place in a jurisdiction like that, felony murder and, hence, first degree murder, probably does exist. As discussed previously in Problem 12.2, robbery is likely a sufficient triggering felony, as is attempted robbery, and the elements of that offense were clearly present here. *See* Chapter 7 (Attempt) & Chapter 13 (Theft).

■ PROBLEM 12.4 ■

[*Reconsider here Problem 3.1, taken from Chapter 3 (Mens Rea), set out below:*]

Eldon Jeffries has been charged with first-degree murder in the death of Karen Hite, a six year-old child. In this jurisdiction, first-degree murder includes the mens rea element of purposeful conduct, as defined by the MPC. What happened was that Jeffries had been drinking heavily at a bar for five hours. He then staggered to his car, got in and drove off wildly and erratically, ultimately speeding right through a red light at sixty m.p.h. and smashing into another car, killing Hite. Is Jeffries guilty of first degree murder?

Analysis

No.

The actus reus of homicide is a killing act resulting in the death of a human being. To commit this act purposefully, Jeffries would have had to have had (under the MPC) the "conscious object to . . . cause such a result." Begging the question for a moment of how "conscious" he actually was due to his heavy drinking, it is clear from these facts that it was not Jeffries' conscious object to crash into the victim's car and kill her. Accordingly, he is not guilty of first-degree murder. Of course, he could well be guilty of a different homicide crime, involuntary manslaughter perhaps, which usually has a mens rea of recklessness.

Then there's the question of the relevance of Jeffries' probable intoxication. *See* Chapter 3 (Mens Rea). Of course, he doesn't need an intoxication defense to negative mens rea, as it is already clear that he has not acted purposefully in any event, as discussed above. But let's change the facts a little bit. Suppose that—in his drunken state—he saw little Karen in her car seat in the car and plowed right into her, intending to kill her for some irrational reason. Hence, his conduct was purposeful, unlike the initial facts. Could he defend on the basis of intoxication? The answer is "yes" . . . but, assuming two things.

First, does this jurisdiction accept intoxication as a defense? If it doesn't, that's the end of this inquiry, of course. But let's assume for the sake of argument that it does.

Then, second, was he sufficiently intoxicated, not just tipsy, but so inebriated that he really couldn't possess the appropriate mens rea for this crime? If not, the inquiry is over once again. But let's assume once again that he was. Let's assume that he just polished off a fifth of gin, four beers, and two cosmopolitans with tiny pink umbrellas in them and pretty much no longer knew what planet he inhabited.

Well, then we're left with the final question: is first degree murder a specific intent crime? If so (and assuming, again, positive answers to the two additional points addressed in the prior paragraphs), then Jeffries does have a good intoxication defense to first degree murder. And first degree murder *is* considered a specific intent crime because the actor's intention goes beyond the assaultive conduct being committed and includes the further intention that that conduct result in the victim's death.

Finally, and once again, it is important to note that the fact that Jeffries may not be guilty of first degree murder due to his intoxication, does not absolve him necessarily of his potential culpability for other homicide offenses which are not specific intent crimes.

POINTS TO REMEMBER

- Presence or absence of malice is line between murder and manslaughter.
- Homicide conviction requires proof of killing act, causation, death of human, and specified mens rea.
- Murder requires proof of malice aforethought, express or implied.

- Malice aforethought is often implied from gross recklessness or extreme indifference to value of human life.
- First degree murder requires proof of premeditation and deliberation.
- In most jurisdictions, no time is too short to establish an accused person's premeditation and deliberation.
- Premeditation and deliberation can be established by prior planning activity, prior relationship with victim, motive, and manner of killing.
- Second degree murder requires proof of malice only, no premeditation and deliberation.
- Felony murder requires proof of independent triggering felony and death during felony, attempted felony or flight after felony.
- Felony murder may not apply to unforeseeable killing by co-felon or third party.
- Voluntary manslaughter is mitigated murder and is usually raised as a mitigating provocation defense.
- Provocation defense is sudden, intense passion from reasonable provocation by victim so serious it would create passion in reasonable person.
- No provocation defense where reasonable cooling-off period existed.
- Voluntary manslaughter can be established by imperfect defense where complete protective defense fails because belief in need to kill deemed unreasonable.
- Involuntary manslaughter is unintentional killing without malice with usual mens rea of gross negligence.

CHAPTER 13

Theft

Theft law is quite different today than it was at common law. Common law theft crimes had a very narrow and limited application, and often consisted of a set of complicated and arcane elements. In contrast, modern theft crimes tend collectively to cover significantly more larcenous conduct and to have clearer and less confusing elements.

A. TRADITIONAL THEFT CRIMES

It was often difficult to prosecute and convict an accused person of one of the common law theft crimes because some of the elements of those crimes were either overly constricted and/or applied in a peculiar fashion.

Moreover, if a prosecutor charged a person with commission of a specific theft crime, the accused was not guilty if the evidence actually adduced at trial showed that he or she was guilty instead of a different type of theft crime.

1. Larceny

In general. Common law larceny was:

- the wrongful taking and carrying away
- of personal property
- in the possession of another person
- with the intent to convert it or to deprive its possessor of the property
- permanently.

Larceny was punishable by death.

Personal property only. Larceny only applied to personal property, not to real or intangible property. It also did not apply to the theft of services (as theft crimes do today). Wild animals could not be stolen either, but domesticated animals could be.

Custody vs. possession. Larceny at common law only applied to trespassory takings, trespassing on the possessory rights of another person.

Significantly, if property was simply in the "custody" of another person, rather than being in the "possession" of another person, the common law crime of larceny was not made out. A person was said to be in custody of property when he or she had temporary control over it, but his or her right to use it was restricted legally by someone else.

A bank teller taking money from the cash drawer would be guilty of larceny as the money was possessed by the bank. A bank teller taking money given to him or her by a depositor without putting it in the cash drawer would not be guilty of larceny because the bank in that case was deemed never to have possessed the money.

Breaking bulk. At common law, a bailee who took all of the goods with which he or she was entrusted was deemed not to be guilty of larceny because the bailee was said to only have had custody not possession of the goods.

But if the bailee only took *some* of the goods, this was called "breaking bulk," and the fiction was adopted that this act caused the bailee to lose possession of them. As a result, he or she was considered guilty of larceny.

Lost property. Lost property that clearly belonged to someone else was treated at common law as if the owner was still in possession of it. This is sometimes called "constructive possession." As a result, a person who found such property and took it, intending to keep it (rather than to return it to the owner), was guilty of larceny.

Where, however, it was not evident that the found property belonged to someone else, e.g. a coin simply lying on the ground, the act of picking it up and taking it was not larceny.

Carrying away: asportation requirement. Larceny required not only a taking at common law, but also the further act of moving the property by carrying it away. This is called the "asportation requirement." Very little actual movement, however, was required to satisfy this element; even a few inches sufficed.

In many American jurisdictions, this asportation requirement was subsequently watered down significantly or eliminated altogether. Today, the appropriate question to be answered is typically simply whether the accused took control of and dominion over the property.

Mens rea. To establish larceny, the accused had to take the item in question with the specific intent to convert it or to permanently deprive the owner of it. "Permanent" included an unreasonably long period of time.

Accordingly, if a person took something with the reasonable intent to return it later—just to borrow it perhaps—that was not larceny. It was also not larceny if the person took something with the reasonable belief that he or she had a lawful claim to it at that time.

Grand vs. petty larceny. The common law distinguished between more serious (sometimes called "grand larceny") and less serious (then called "petit larceny," now called "petty larceny") larceny crimes, by focusing on the value of the property taken. This same distinction is often still made today.

Modern statutes. Today, most jurisdictions' crimes codes contain a basic and much more inclusive theft crime that covers all forms and manner of the unlawful misappropriation of the property of another person. Modern theft offenses tend not to have all—or, at least, to have fewer—of the confusing distinctions and elements found at common law.

In addition, newer forms of larcenous conduct have been criminalized, e.g. theft of wireless communications, theft of utilities, identity theft, and shoplifting.

2. Larceny by Trick

Common law. It was the separate offense of larceny by trick where a person gained possession of—but not title to—property from its owner by means of fraud or false pretenses.

However, larceny by trick required proof that the accused intended to act fraudulently from the very beginning, at the moment when he or she took the property in question. Where a person rented property but only later decided not to return it, for example, that was held not to be larceny by trick as the initial possession of the property was not considered larcenous.

Modern statutes. Today, most jurisdictions do not use these arcane distinctions. Crimes codes include theft crimes that apply simply and specifically to a renter's failure to return rental property.

3. Embezzlement

Early law. Beginning in the late eighteenth century, it was the crime of embezzlement when a person fraudulently converted the property of another person while he or she was in lawful possession of that property. Some embezzlement statutes also required proof that the accused gained possession of the property from or for the benefit of the owner of the property.

Embezzlement was a specific intent crime. If the property was taken pursuant to a mistaken belief that the taker owned it, for example, the crime of embezzlement was not made out.

Compared to larceny. It was embezzlement when an actor possessed property lawfully but then converted it fraudulently; it was larceny when an actor wrongfully took property in the possession of another.

Modern statutes. Today, many jurisdictions have enacted crimes relating to theft by failure to make required disposition of funds which apply to takings by persons who have obtained property subject to a known obligation to do something with it, but use it for themselves instead of meeting that obligation. *See* Model Penal Code (MPC) § 223.8. It no longer matters who had formal possession of the property when it was obtained.

4. False Pretenses

Early law. It was the crime of false pretenses where a person:

- knowingly
- misrepresented material facts
- in order to and with the result of defrauding another person into giving him or her title to that person's property.

Not only must such misrepresentations have been false, but the person accused must have been shown to have known that they were false, i.e. it need to be demonstrated that the accused was acting with the intent to defraud.

Omissions. It was deemed not to be a misrepresentation for a person simply to fail to disclose information. Only affirmative misrepresentations could lead to a false pretenses conviction. Additionally, false pretenses did not include misrepresentations or exaggerations as to the value of property.

Compared to larceny by trick. It was false pretenses to fraudulently obtain title to property; it was larceny by trick to fraudulently obtain possession of property.

Modern statutes. Today, many jurisdictions have combined the crimes of false pretenses and larceny by trick into a broader theft by deception crime.

B. MODERN CONSOLIDATION OF THEFT CRIMES

Model Penal Code. The MPC addressed the common law's confusing array of convoluted theft crimes by "consolidating" the most common separate crimes at common law into one single, inclusive theft offense. This consolidated theft-crime approach is followed today in a majority of states.

Consolidation. The MPC consolidated into one theft crime the commission of any of the following larcenous acts:

- theft by unlawful taking or disposition;
- theft by deception;
- theft by extortion;
- theft of property lost, mislaid, or delivered by mistake;
- receiving stolen property;
- theft of services;
- theft by failure to make required disposition of funds received;
- and unauthorized use of automobiles and other vehicles.

These various types of theft—now consolidated into one crime—include a broad range of conduct with the unifying theme that they all involve the unlawful taking of the property of other persons.

Under MPC § 223.2, for example, it is theft by unlawful taking or disposition if a person "unlawfully takes, or exercises unlawful control over, movable property of another with purpose to deprive him thereof [or] unlawfully transfers immovable property of another or any interest therein with purpose to benefit himself or another not entitled thereto."

Variance in proof at trial. Unlike the common law, if the prosecution prosecutes a person for one of these types of theft set out above, but the evidence at trial establishes a different type of theft (that is also covered by applicable law), that person is still guilty of theft under this consolidated statute. Most jurisdictions in the United States now use this consolidated theft-crime approach.

Most jurisdictions—and the MPC—do, however, still distinguish between these different types of theft for purposes of assessing post-conviction sentences, i.e. these different theft offenses carry varying degrees and levels of punishment.

C. RECEIVING STOLEN PROPERTY

The crime of receiving stolen property is committed when a person:

- gains control over property
- believing that it was obtained criminally
- intending to deprive its owner of his or her interest in it
- permanently.

Stolen property. At common law, this crime did not apply to property which was given to someone by another person when that person was cooperating with the police and had not actually stolen it.

But MPC § 223.6(1) provides that defendants can be convicted of receiving stolen property if they receive it "believing that it has probably been stolen, unless the property is received . . . with purpose to restore it to the owner." This MPC approach is the rule in most states today.

Even where a jurisdiction still follows the common law, however, such a person would likely be guilty of the crime of attempted receiving stolen property. *See* Chapter 7 (Attempt).

Presumption. MPC § 223.6(2) contains a presumption that a person knew or believed that property was stolen where he or she: "(a) is found in possession or control of property stolen from two or more persons on separate occasions; (b) has received stolen property in another transaction within the year preceding the transaction charged; or (c) being a dealer in property of the sort received, acquires it for a consideration which he knows is far below its reasonable value."

Many crimes codes contain a similar presumption. Even where no presumption exists, a person's knowledge or belief that property was stolen can be—and often is—established circumstantially.

D. OTHER TAKINGS OFFENSES

Many jurisdictions have dozens of crimes on the books other than strict theft crimes that also relate to unlawful takings from other people. These additional crimes invariably include robbery and burglary in every jurisdiction.

1. Robbery

Robbery is a more serious offense than theft. It focuses on the use or threat of violence or force when a theft of property is committed.

Common law. Under the common law, robbery was larceny that included a taking from the person or in the presence of the victim that was accomplished by violence or a threat of violence. *See, e.g., Stokeling v. United States*, 139 S. Ct. 544, 550 (2019) ("At common law, an unlawful taking was merely larceny unless the crime involved 'violence.' . . . And 'violence' was 'committed if sufficient force [was] exerted to overcome the resistance encountered.' ").

Model Penal Code. Robbery is a separate criminal offense under the MPC and in jurisdictions with consolidated theft crimes.

MPC § 222.1(1) does not, however, require that the taking be from or in the presence of the victim. Rather, "a person is guilty of robbery if, in the course of committing a theft, he: (a) inflicts serious bodily injury upon another; or (b) threatens another with or purposely puts him in fear of immediate serious bodily injury; or (c) commits or threatens immediately to commit any felony of the first or second degree."

Robbery statutes in most states are to similar effect.

Moreover, with respect to the common law robbery offense, "there will be cases, appropriately reached by a charge of attempted robbery, where the actor does not actually harm anyone or even threaten harm. If, for example, the defendant is apprehended before he reaches his robbery victim and thus before he has actually engaged in threatening conduct, proof of his purpose to engage in such conduct can justify a conviction of attempted robbery so long as his intention and some other substantial step are present." *United States v. Taylor*, 142 S. Ct. 2015, 2020–21 (2022).

Armed robbery. Armed robbery is an aggravated form of robbery which is punished more severely than the basic robbery offense. It is often defined as a robbery which is committed while the person committing it possessed a deadly weapon, like a gun or a knife.

Carjacking. Carjacking is another aggravated form of robbery which is generally punished much more severely. Carjacking is essentially a robbery where a victim's car is taken from him or her by force.

2. Burglary

Common law. Burglary at common law was committed when a person:

- broke and entered into
- another person's dwelling

- at night with the specific intent to commit a felony inside.

See, e.g., Quarles v. U.S., 139 S. Ct. 1872, 1876 (2019) ("At common law, burglary was confined to unlawful breaking and entering a dwelling at night with the intent to commit a felony.").

Model Penal Code. MPC § 221.1(1) provides, in relevant part, that a person has committed the crime of burglary if "he enters a building or occupied structure . . . with purpose to commit a crime therein, unless the premises are at the time open to the public or the actor is licensed or privileged to enter."

Modern statutes. Today, the crime of burglary in most jurisdictions is similar to the MPC approach, generally applicable to entries at any time of the night or day, and to entries not just into dwellings, but into any buildings or occupied structures. *See United States v. Stitt*, 139 S. Ct. 399, 405 (2018) ("[M]ost States ha[ve] expanded the meaning of burglary to include 'structures other than dwellings.' ").

License or privilege. Most jurisdictions, like the MPC, do not extend the crime of burglary to a person's entry into a place that he or she is either licensed or privileged to enter.

Such license or privilege does not mean that the person must be an owner of the property in question. Usually, a person is considered to be privileged to enter a place where he could reasonably be expected to be present.

THEFT CHECKLIST

A. **Traditional Theft Crimes**—complicated and arcane elements.

1. **Larceny**—wrongful taking and carrying away of personal property in possession of another with intent to convert it or to deprive possessor of it permanently.

   a. **Personal Property Only**—larceny inapplicable to real or intangible property, theft of services, or wild animals.

   b. **Trespass on Possession**—larceny only applied to trespassing on possession of another.

      i. **Not Custody**—not larceny to take property only in custody of another.

ii. **Custody Defined**—temporary control over property where right of use restricted legally by another.

c. **Breaking Bulk**—bailee taking all bailed goods not guilty of larceny; bailee taking only some bailed goods was "breaking bulk," and was guilty of larceny.

d. **Lost Property**—if clearly belonged to someone else, finder who took it, intending to keep it, was guilty of larceny.

i. **Return to Owner**—not larceny if finder intended to return it to owner.

ii. **No Clear Owner**—not larceny where not clear that lost property belonged to someone else.

e. **Asportation**—larceny requires movement "carrying away" beyond mere taking.

i. **Little Movement Required**—movement even of inches sufficed.

ii. **Today**—question is generally only whether control and dominion over property.

f. **Mens Rea**—specific intent to convert or permanently deprive owner of property.

i. **Permanent**—includes unreasonably long period of time.

ii. **Return or Claim**—not larceny if reasonable intent to return property later or reasonable belief in claim to it.

g. **Grand vs. Petty**—grand (serious) and petty (less serious) larceny distinguished usually by value of property taken.

2. **Larceny by Trick**—gaining possession of property from owner by fraud or false pretenses.

a. **Mens Rea**—intent to act fraudulently when property taken.

b. **Rentals**—treated differently.

i. **Older View**—not larceny by trick if person decided not to return property after it was taken.

ii. **Newer View**—failure to return rental property criminal.

3. **Embezzlement**—fraudulently converting property of another person while in lawful possession of it.
   a. **Mens Rea**—specific intent; not crime if taker mistakenly believed owned it.
   b. **Different from Larceny**—embezzlement when possessed property lawfully but then converted fraudulently; larceny when wrongfully took property in possession of another.
   c. **Today**—theft by failure to make required disposition of funds: taking by person who obtained property subject to known obligation but used it for self instead.
4. **False Pretenses**—knowingly misrepresenting material facts to and with the result of defrauding another person into transferring title to his or her property.
   a. **Mens Rea**—knowledge that representations were false, i.e. intent to defraud.
   b. **Limited Misrepresentations**—does not include failure to disclose information or misrepresentations or exaggerations as to value of property.
   c. **Different from Larceny by Trick**—false pretenses to fraudulently obtain title; larceny by trick to fraudulently obtain mere possession.
   d. **Today**—false pretenses and larceny by trick often combined into theft by deception.

B. **Consolidation of Theft Offenses**—majority consolidate separate theft crimes into one inclusive theft offense.
   1. **Variances in Evidence at Trial Okay**—theft established if prosecution for one included type of theft, but proof establishes different included type of theft.
   2. **Grading**—punishment for different types of theft still different.

C. **Receiving Stolen Property**—gaining control over property believing it was obtained criminally, intending to permanently deprive owner of interest in it.
   1. **Undercover Stings**—even if property not really stolen, still crime if accused believed it was; changed common law rule.
   2. **Presumption**—knowledge that property stolen often presumed where person found in possession of stolen

property from many people, prior receipt of such property, or dealer getting property he or she knows below reasonable value.

D. **Robbery**—theft with use or threat of violence or force.

   1. **Common Law**—larceny with taking from or in presence of person accomplished by violence or threat of violence.

   2. **Today**—theft where serious bodily injury inflicted or threatened, victim put in fear of such injury, or serious felony threatened.

E. **Burglary**—theft in a building.

   1. **Common Law**—breaking and entering into another's dwelling at night with specific intent to commit a felony inside.

   2. **Today**—entering a building or occupied structure intending to commit a crime inside.

      a. **Time of Day**—irrelevant.

      b. **License or Privilege**—not burglary where person licensed or privileged to enter premises.

ILLUSTRATIVE PROBLEMS

The following problems illustrate how the checklist points help to resolve questions relating to theft crimes.

■ PROBLEM 13.1 ■

Louis Higgins asked Bonnie Karlen one Friday morning if he could borrow her car to drive to the Los Angeles airport and pick up his friend, a former college roommate, that afternoon. Karlen agreed, but told Higgins to have the car back by 6:00 that evening because she needed it to drive to her mother's house for dinner. Higgins agreed, having every intention of doing just that.

Higgins took the car and did pick up his friend at the LA airport. But his friend then suggested that they get right back into the car and drive to Las Vegas for the evening and gamble. Although that is not what Higgins had planned to do, that is in fact exactly what the two of them did do.

As a result, Higgins did not return the car to Karlen until Sunday afternoon. Karlen, not surprisingly, was boiling mad at Higgins for not returning her car when he had agreed to return it, since he knew full well that she needed it on Friday.

Was Higgins guilty of a common law or traditional theft crime?

Analysis

No.

Higgins was not guilty of common law larceny as he was in possession of the property and he did not have the intent to convert it or to deprive Karlen of it permanently. Similarly, Higgins was not guilty of embezzlement because he did not fraudulently convert Karlen's property—her car—while he was in possession of it.

Higgins was also not guilty of common law larceny by trick as he did not gain possession of the car from Karlen by means of fraud or false pretenses. At the time that he borrowed her car, he genuinely intended to return it as agreed. It was only later, at the airport, that he decided—*what the hell!*—to use the car to drive to Las Vegas with his friend.

Nor was Higgins guilty of the crime of false pretenses as he did not knowingly misrepresent any material facts to Karlen in order to and with the result of defrauding her person into giving him title to her car.

Parenthetically, Higgins would likely have been guilty of a crime in most jurisdictions today, under modern crimes codes. Most jurisdictions have some sort of car theft statute, criminalizing the act of using someone else's car without that person's consent and without a reasonable belief that the owner would have consented to the use.

These sorts of statutes reach well beyond the common law theft offenses, as you can see from the discussion above. They apply to conduct that was not meant to deprive the owner of her vehicle permanently, and it does not matter whether or not the person taking the vehicle has a fraudulent intent.

■ PROBLEM 13.2 ■

Paul Dell held a realistic-looking water pistol on Sara Maritato and told her that he would "mess her up bad" if Maritato didn't hand her purse over to him. Maritato didn't hesitate. She immediately handed Dell her purse.

Once Dell took the purse from her, he ran away. After reaching a secluded spot, he pulled Maritato's' wallet out of the purse, and pocketed all of the cash and credit cards. He then pulled out Maritato's' driver's license and wrote down the address on it: 223 Beech Street #1.

Dell immediately headed toward Beech Street to see what he could find inside Maritato's apartment to add to his haul. When Dell arrived at the apartment building at 223 Beech, he pushed all of the intercom buzzers until someone buzzed him in. He then broke the lock on the door to Apartment #1, entered, and found and removed some jewelry, audio equipment, and a large, flat-screen TV set.

Actually, the apartment that Dell entered belonged to Talia Cooper, not to Maritato. Maritato had moved out of the apartment months before but had neglected to change the address on her driver's license.

His image recorded on the entry door camera, Dell was quickly identified and apprehended. What crimes, if any, has Dell committed?

Analysis

Dell is guilty of robbery, assault, burglary, and theft.

Dell is guilty of robbery as, in the course of committing a theft, he threatened Maritato with and/or likely put her in fear of (an alternate element) immediate serious bodily injury when he pointed what looked to be a gun at her and said he would "mess her up bad." He is not guilty of armed robbery, however, as he was not actually armed with a deadly weapon.

Dell is also guilty of assault. *See* Chapter 10 (Assault). Although not covered in this Chapter, Dell intentionally placed Maritato in fear of an imminent battery.

Dell committed a burglary as well. He entered a building he was not licensed or privileged to enter with the intent to commit a crime—theft, see below—inside. If the jurisdiction in which these events occurred requires that the intended crime be a felony, it is very likely that the value of the items taken would insure that that element was satisfied. Moreover, it makes no difference at all that Dell was not in the apartment that he intended to be in. He still entered someone else's apartment without lawful right or permission to do so with the intent to steal something from inside.

Finally, Dell was also guilty of theft. In MPC terms, he was guilty of theft by unlawful taking or disposition as he unlawfully took Cooper's moveable property with the purpose to deprive her thereof.

POINTS TO REMEMBER

- Traditional larceny is wrongful taking and carrying away of personal property in possession of another with intent to convert it or deprive possessor of it permanently.
- Traditionally, not larceny to take property only in custody not possession of another.

- Traditionally, bailee is not guilty of larceny unless "breaking bulk."
- Traditionally, finder of lost property is guilty of larceny if it clearly belonged to someone else and finder intended to keep it.
- Traditionally, larceny by trick was gaining possession of property from its owner by fraud or false pretenses.
- Traditionally, embezzlement was fraudulently converting property of another while in lawful possession of that property.
- Traditionally, false pretenses was knowingly misrepresenting material facts to and with the result of defrauding another person into transferring title to his or her property.
- Majority of jurisdictions today consolidate separate theft crimes into one inclusive theft offense.
- Theft is established today in most states if proof is of one type of covered theft, although prosecution for another.
- Receiving stolen property is gaining control over property believing it was obtained criminally, intending to permanently deprive owner of interest in it.
- Knowledge that property was stolen can be presumed from presence of stolen goods from number of people, prior acts of receiving such goods, or dealers getting goods far below value.
- Robbery today is theft where serious bodily injury inflicted or threatened, victim put in fear of such injury, or serious felony threatened.
- Burglary today is entering a building or occupied structure intending to commit a crime inside.

CHAPTER 14

Justification Defenses

Justification defenses are criminal law defenses permitted in order to allow a person to make an appropriate response to certain external events. Excuse defenses, in contrast, *see* Chapter 15 (Excuses), are criminal law defenses accepted because the person acting is deemed not to be blameworthy for some appropriate reason. Or you can simply look at this distinction this way:

- justifications = external issues;
- excuses = internal issues.

Affirmative defenses. Justification defenses are usually "affirmative defenses." This means that they do not depend upon defense counsel negativing (by creating a reasonable doubt as to) one of the elements of a crime. Instead, even if all of those elements have been proved, a defendant may defend affirmatively by proving the separate elements of an affirmative defense set out by statute.

Ordinarily, the burden of proof on a defendant for making an affirmative defense is proof by a preponderance of the evidence.

A. SELF DEFENSE

Self defense is a defense to criminal charges that recognizes a person's right to defend himself or herself from attack, provided that certain important requirements are met, as set out below. *McDonald v. City of Chicago, Ill.*, 561 U.S. 742, 767 (2010) ("Self-defense is a basic right, recognized by many legal systems from ancient times to the present day . . . ."). This defense is used most commonly in homicide prosecutions, *see* Chapter 12 (Homicide), but applies as well to other assault or attempted homicide or sex crimes. *See, e.g.*, Chapter 7 (Attempt), Chapter 10 (Assault), Chapter 11 (Sex Crimes).

Basic test. The typical elements of self defense are as follows: A person

- who is not an aggressor

- may use otherwise unlawful force (but not deadly force, *see* below)
- to protect himself or herself against an attack by another person
- when he or she reasonably believes that he or she is threatened
- with the imminent use of unlawful force
- and that force is necessary to repel that attack.

1. Honest & Reasonable Belief

The use of defensive force is available only when the person using it *reasonably* believes that he or she is threatened with the imminent use of unlawful force and that the use of responsive force is necessary to repel that attack.

Subjective and objective components. This is a test with both subjective and objective components. The person using defensive force must honestly believe these things (that there is an imminent threat of unlawful force and that the use of responsive force is necessary). This is the subjective component.

That belief (that there is an imminent threat of unlawful force and that the use of responsive force is necessary) does not need to be correct. But it must be reasonable. That reasonableness element is the objective component of the test.

Where a person has an honest belief that there is an imminent threat of unlawful force and that the use of responsive force is necessary, but that belief is objectively unreasonable, a self-defense affirmative defense cannot lawfully be made out. However, in many jurisdictions, in homicide cases, that showing would be enough to make a mitigating "imperfect defense" entitling a killer to a verdict of voluntary manslaughter. *See* discussion below.

Reasonable compared to whom? Ordinarily, we gauge reasonableness by asking what a reasonable person would have done. In most jurisdictions, in this setting, an accused person's physical characteristics, e.g. his or her disability or age, may be considered by jurors today in deciding whether or not that person acted reasonably in using protective force under the circumstances. If the accused is blind, for example, would a reasonable blind person have responded in the way that she did when her cane was grabbed from her?

But most jurisdictions do not permit a jury to consider an accused person's mental or emotional characteristics or views, e.g. his or her hot temper or his or her extreme hatred of some group of individuals. We do *not* ask the jury, for example, whether a reasonable, hot-tempered person would have reacted as this accused, hot-tempered person did.

2. Necessity & Imminency

In general. A person is not entitled to use defensive force unless the threat of unlawful force against him or her is imminent and it is necessary to respond.

Someone's threat to leave and return with a gun or knife to use it against a person at a later time does not, for example, justify that person's present use of immediate force in self defense. The use of force threatened against him or her was not imminent; nor was it necessary to respond with force immediately for purposes of self protection.

Or, viewed another way, imminency is often simply another way to establish necessity: When danger is not imminent, it is not necessary to act.

Waiting to act. Despite the imminency requirement, a person is not required to wait until the very last possible second before using force in self defense. The inquiry, as noted previously, is whether and when the person acting had an honest and reasonable belief that an imminent threat of unlawful force existed and that the use of responsive force was necessary for protective purposes.

Battered spouse defense. The requirements of imminency and necessity often make it difficult if not impossible for a physically abused spouse (or partner) to use a self-defense defense when he or she has responded to that abuse with force (often killing the abuser).

In many cases, abused spouses have attacked their abusing spouse at a moment when they have the physical ability to do so, e.g., when the abusing spouse is asleep. At such a moment, however, the threat of unlawful force against the abused spouse is not imminent. Nor is it necessary to respond to such abuse at that very moment. As a result, the defense of self defense is usually deemed to be inapplicable.

Expert testimony. Some jurisdictions have permitted homicide defendants to introduce expert testimony, where applicable, about "battered spouse (sometimes called "battered wife") syndrome." Such experts generally explain that a cycle of violence exists in many domestic abuse cases that creates "learned helplessness" and affects the abused spouse's ability to react to violence when it occurs, and that such abuse victims may have greater sensitivity to assessing the risk of violence where its imminent use might appear less likely to an outsider.

Where permitted, this testimony is deemed admissible for the purpose of assisting jurors in assessing a battered spouse's honest and reasonable belief about imminency and necessity.

3. Aggressors

An aggressor is not entitled to use the defense of self defense. An aggressor is an individual who has threatened or initiated the unlawful use of force against someone else.

An aggressor may, however, regain self defense rights if his or her victim responds to an attack by using excessive force. This possibility is discussed below with respect to the use of deadly force.

4. Unlawful Arrest

Under the common law, a person had the right to use force (but not deadly force) to resist an unlawful arrest being made by a police officer. In some jurisdictions today, a minority, a person still has this right.

But in other jurisdictions, a majority today, there is no right to use force to resist an unlawful arrest. Model Penal Code (MPC) § 3.04(2)(a)(i) takes this approach, providing that "[t]he use of force is not justifiable . . . to resist an arrest which the actor knows is being made by a peace officer, although the arrest is unlawful."

However, this majority rule does not prohibit using force to respond to a police officer who uses excessive force in making a stop or an arrest. *See* the discussion of excessive force in the next section relating to the use of deadly force.

5. Deadly Force

What is it? In general, deadly force is the use of force that is intended or likely to cause death or serious bodily injury.

MPC § 3.11(2) defines "deadly force" as, *inter alia*, "force which the actor uses with the purpose of causing or which he knows to create a substantial risk of causing death or serious bodily harm."

The use of a firearm or knife, for example, are classic examples of the use of deadly force.

Model Penal Code. MPC § 3.04(2)(b) provides that "[t]he use of deadly force is not justifiable . . . unless the actor believes that such force is necessary to protect himself against death, serious bodily harm, kidnapping or sexual intercourse compelled by force or threat."

While they do not all use the same list of threatened offenses, most jurisdictions take much the same approach to the use of deadly force as the MPC.

Proportionality. In essence, a person may respond to the use of force against himself or herself with force, and may respond to the use of deadly force against himself or herself with deadly force.

A person's response to a physical threat must therefore be proportional to the amount of force with which he or she is threatened. A person is never entitled, for example, to use deadly force to respond to a non-deadly attack.

a. Aggressors

An aggressor is not entitled to use deadly force in self defense. As MPC § 3.04(2)(b)(i) provides, "[t]he use of deadly force is not . . . justifiable if . . . the actor, with the purpose of causing death or serious bodily harm, provoked the use of force against himself in the same encounter."

This approach is similar to that taken in most jurisdictions.

i. Withdrawals

An initial aggressor can, however, regain the right to use deadly force in self defense if he or she withdraws from the fray, other than temporarily or strategically, and makes it clear that he or she has withdrawn.

ii. Excessive Force

An initial aggressor is entitled to use force in self-defense when a person he has initially attacked responds to that attack with excessive force, i.e. force beyond that which he or she was lawfully entitled to use.

Most commonly, this entitlement applies in a case where an initial aggressor has used unlawful force and his or her victim has responded to that unlawful force with deadly force. Since the victim did not have the right to use deadly force in responding to the use of mere force, the initial aggressor regains his or her self defense rights. The initial aggressor can then respond to the use of excessive force against him or her with force or deadly force, as the circumstances would permit.

b. Retreat Doctrine

Common law. Under the common law, a person being attacked by another person was not required to retreat before using deadly force in his or her defense.

Model Penal Code. Unlike the common law, MPC § 3.04(b)(ii) provides that the use of deadly force in self defense is not justifiable where "the actor knows that he can avoid the necessity of using such force with complete safety by retreating or by surrendering possession of a thing to a person asserting a claim of right thereto or by complying with a demand that he abstain from any action which he has no duty to take."

Today. Some jurisdictions still follow the common-law approach, but many jurisdictions today follow the MPC approach and accept the "retreat doctrine."

i. Castle Doctrine

Most jurisdictions applying the retreat doctrine, also recognize an exception to it where the person using force in self defense is acting in his or her own home (viz. "a man's [*sic*] home is his castle"). This exception is often extended as well to a person's place of work. Some jurisdictions have more recently extended this no-retreat, "stand your ground" exception farther still, e.g. to someone being forcefully dispossessed from his or her vehicle.

Exceptions to the exception. The castle doctrine is held to be inapplicable in some jurisdictions where the person seeking to use it was the initial aggressor, or where that person was using force in his or her home or workplace against a co-habitant or co-worker. In other words, in these cases, because there is an exception to the castle doctrine, the retreat doctrine continues to apply.

MPC § 3.04(b)(ii)(1) takes just this approach (except as to co-habitants), providing that a person "is not obliged to retreat from his dwelling or place of work, unless he was the initial aggressor or is assailed in his place of work by another person whose place of work the actor knows it to be."

Battered spouses. In some jurisdictions, battered spouses have been held not to have retreat obligations even though they used deadly force against a co-habitant, where that co-habitant was the abusing spouse.

ii. Complete Safety

The retreat doctrine is inapplicable where the person using deadly force is unable to retreat in complete safety, e.g. another person is aiming a loaded gun at him or her and there is no place nor time to run or hide.

B. DEFENSE OF OTHERS

Common law. Under the common law, a person was permitted to use otherwise unlawful force not only for self-protection, but in defense of close relatives as well. Today, this defense of others is rarely so limited.

Alter ego rule. A minority of jurisdictions today provide that a right to act in defense of others is limited by the other person's actual right of self defense. This is the "alter ego" rule. Using this approach, the person using force metaphorically "steps into the shoes" of the person being attacked. If that person had the right of self defense, then the person using force has the same right.

The problem with this rule is that if the person using force to defend another is wrong about the perceived victim's right to use self defense, then the use of force to protect that person is not justifiable. That is true even though the person using it may have thought that he or she was doing the right thing.

Model Penal Code. In contrast to the alter ego rule, MPC § 3.05(1) provides that "the use of force upon or toward the person of another is justifiable to protect a third person when: (a) the actor would be justified . . . in using such force to protect himself against the injury he believes to be threatened to the person whom he seeks to protect; and (b) under the circumstances as the actor believes them to be the person whom he seeks to protect would be justified in using such protective force; and (c) the actor believes that his intervention is necessary for the protection of such other person."

The key difference between the alter ego rule and the MPC rule is that the latter turns on the point of view of the person using the force rather than the point of view of the person who is being threatened or assaulted. Under the MPC approach, if the person using force honestly believes that the use of force is justified and necessary under the circumstances, it is lawful.

Most jurisdictions today hold that if a person reasonably believes that the use of protective force is justified and necessary under the circumstances because of a threat or assault on another person (whether or not that person is a close relative), such use of otherwise unlawful force is lawful.

Retreat. In jurisdictions where the retreat doctrine exists, it does not apply to the defense of others unless the person using the force *and* the person who is being defended both can retreat in complete safety.

C. DEFENSE OF PROPERTY OR HABITATION

Common law. Under the common law, a person could use unlawful force to protect his or her personal or real property when he or she reasonably believed the use of such force was immediately necessary.

The use of deadly force was only permissible in this setting, however, where the person using it reasonably believed it was necessary to prevent an imminent and unlawful, forcible entry into his or her dwelling.

Model Penal Code. MPC § 3.06(1)(a) permits the use of force when a person believes that it is necessary to prevent or terminate an unlawful trespass or the unlawful carrying away of property.

The use of force is also lawful, under MPC § 3.06(1)(b),where a person seeks to re-enter or retake his or her property if the force is used immediately after the property was taken and the person believes that the person who has entered or taken the property has no rightful claim to possession of it.

In either event, under MPC § 3.06(3), the person using force must first make a request for the property unless such request would be useless or dangerous.

Most jurisdictions today hold similarly that the use of force is lawful when a person reasonably believes that it is necessary to prevent or terminate an unlawful trespass or the unlawful carrying away of property.

Deadly force. The MPC prohibits the use of deadly force to protect property, except in exceptional circumstances. These exceptional circumstances include the use of deadly force:

- to prevent being thrown out of one's dwelling, MPC § 3.06(3)(d)(i),
- and to prevent arson, burglary, robbery or other felonious theft or property destruction, where the person the force is to be used against employed or threatened deadly force, or the use of force other than deadly force "would expose the actor or another in his presence to substantial danger of serious bodily harm," MPC § 3.06(3)(d)(ii).

Defense of habitation. Most jurisdictions today permit the use of deadly force by a homeowner to prevent or terminate an unlawful entry into the homeowner's dwelling when he or she reasonably believes that the intruder intends to commit a felony inside the home.

But some jurisdictions are more permissive, also permitting the use of deadly force when there has been an unlawful entry into a person's dwelling and he or she reasonably believes that nothing less than deadly force would be adequate to terminate that entry. In such jurisdictions, the intruder's intent—what he or she planned to do inside the dwelling—is irrelevant.

Trap guns. The use of trap guns (sometimes called "spring guns") or other mechanical devices on property that create a "substantial risk of causing death or serious bodily injury" is prohibited by MPC § 3.06(5), and the law in most jurisdictions.

D. IMPERFECT DEFENSES

As noted in Chapter 12 (Homicide), in many jurisdictions, a murder charge can be mitigated to voluntary manslaughter by means of an "imperfect defense."

An imperfect defense is a traditional protective defense like self defense, defense of others, or defense of property or habitation, discussed above, where the accused honestly believed that he or she needed to use deadly force in order to take protective action, but that belief was unreasonable. Put another way, an imperfect defense is made out when a complete protective defense is imperfectly established because every element of that defense was proved except the reasonableness of the person's belief in the imminence of harm and the necessity to act.

Some jurisdictions do not permit an imperfect self-defense where the crime charged requires proof of the mens rea of recklessness or negligence. *See* Chapter 3 (Mens Rea). The MPC takes a similar approach.

E. LAW ENFORCEMENT DEFENSE

Common law. At common law, law enforcement officers could use any force reasonably necessary, including deadly force, to prevent a felony or where they reasonably believed they had probable cause to make a felony arrest. Only non-deadly force could be used to make a misdemeanor arrest, however.

Private citizens assisting officers making such arrests had the same rights as the police officers who they were assisting. But a private citizen acting on his or her own could only use force to make an arrest for a felony, not a misdemeanor.

Model Penal Code. The MPC permits the use of force in making an arrest where the person making the arrest believes its use is immediately necessary. However, the use of deadly force in making an arrest is limited by MPC § 3.07(2)(b) to situations where "(i) the arrest is for a felony; and (ii) the person effecting the arrest is authorized to act as a peace officer or is assisting a person whom he believes to be authorized to act as a peace officer; and (iii) the actor believes that the force employed creates no substantial risk of injury to innocent persons; and (iv) the actor believes that: (1) the crime for which the arrest is made involved conduct including the use or threatened use of deadly force; or (2) there is a substantial risk that the person to be arrested will cause death or serious bodily harm if his apprehension is delayed."

MPC § 3.07(4)(a) permits a private citizen to assist police officers when asked to do so and to use force as long as he or she believes the arrest is lawful.

Most jurisdictions today hold that the use of force by a law enforcement officer to prevent a crime or to make an arrest is lawful when it is reasonably necessary to use such force to make a lawful arrest. Deadly force cannot be used, however, except where the officer reasonably believes that there is a substantial risk that someone committing a crime or being arrested poses a serious danger to himself or others if such force is not used immediately. *See, e.g., Rivas-Villegas v. Cortesluna*, 142 S. Ct. 4, 8 (2021) ("Whether an officer has used excessive force depends on the facts and circumstances of each particular case, including the severity of the crime at issue, whether the suspect poses an immediate threat to the safety of the officers or others, and whether he is actively resisting arrest or attempting to evade arrest by flight.").

Tennessee v. Garner. Similarly, the Supreme Court has held that it is unconstitutional under the Fourth Amendment for a police officer to use deadly force to prevent the escape of a fleeing felon unless it is necessary and the officer has probable cause to believe that that person poses a significant threat of death or serious physical injury to the officer or others. *Tennessee v. Garner*, 471 U.S. 1 (1985). *See also Rivas-Villegas v. Cortesluna*, 142 S. Ct. 4, 8 (2021); *Kisela v. Hughes*, 138 S. Ct. 1148, 1152 (2018).

F. NECESSITY

Traditionally, the necessity defense has permitted a person to commit a crime in order to prevent a greater harm posed by a natural event, e.g. breaking into a building to get out of the path of a tornado. This defense is available in a majority of jurisdictions when a person is faced with an imminent threat of serious injury and has no reasonable, lawful alternative other than to commit a less serious crime to in order to avoid that threat.

Model Penal Code "choice of evils." MPC § 3.02(1) provides that "[c]onduct which the actor believes to be necessary to avoid a harm or evil to himself or to another is justifiable, provided that: (a) the harm or evil sought to be avoided . . . is greater than that sought to be prevented . . .; and (b) neither the Code nor other law defining the offense provides exceptions or defenses dealing with the specific situation involved; and (c) a legislative purpose to exclude the justification claimed does not otherwise plainly appear."

Reckless or negligent conduct. MPC § 3.02(2) excludes use of the choice of evils defense when the person acting was either reckless or negligent and the charged offense has a mens rea of recklessness or negligence. This limitation on necessity is widely followed. In essence, a person may not create the conditions that lead to a necessity defense.

Homicide excluded. Most jurisdictions today do not permit use of a necessity defense in an attempt to justify commission of a homicide.

Objective test. Necessity is judged using an objective test: was the criminal conduct reasonably necessary? A person's subjective belief that it was in fact necessary to avoid a greater evil is not controlling. The focus is upon what a reasonable person in those circumstances would believe.

Necessity vs. duress. Necessity is a justification defense relating to a response to threats from natural events; duress is an excuse, *see* Chapter 15 (Excuses), relating to a response to human threats.

G. CONSENT

Consent of the victim is a valid justification defense for some, but by no means all, criminal offenses.

Most often, this issue arises with respect to physical assaults. *See, e.g.*, Chapter 10 (Assault) and Chapter 11 (Sex Crimes). A person can consent to be cut with a knife by a surgeon, for example, an act which would otherwise be an assaultive crime in the absence of consent. Likewise, a person can consent to participating in a football game, knowing full well that he or she will be hit and tackled repeatedly, acts that would be crimes in the absence of express or implicit consent. But a victim's consent to being killed ("assisted suicide") is usually deemed not to be a valid justification in and of itself for such a homicidal act.

Model Penal Code. MPC § 2.11(1) provides that consent is a defense where it "negatives an element of the offense or precludes the infliction of the harm or evil sought to be prevented by the law defining the offense."

Consent to bodily harm is a defense, under MPC § 2.11(2), if the harm consented to is not serious, or the conduct and the injury are reasonably foreseeable hazards of participating in a lawful athletic event.

MPC § 2.11(3) provides that such consent is ineffective if it is given by someone who is incompetent or who is forced or tricked into consenting.

JUSTIFICATION DEFENSES CHECKLIST

A. **In General**—justification defenses permitted to allow otherwise unlawful response to certain external events.

   1. **Justifications vs. Excuses**—justifications = external issues; excuses = internal issues.

   2. **Affirmative Defenses**—most justification defenses are affirmative defenses.

      a. **Relationship to Proof of Crime**—even if elements of crime proven, defendant may use affirmative defense by proving separate exculpatory elements.

      b. **Burden of Proof**—usually preponderance of evidence not beyond a reasonable doubt.

B. **Self Defense**—commonly used in homicide prosecutions, but applies to other assaultive crimes as well.

   1. **Test**—non-aggressor may use force to protect against attack by another person when reasonable belief threat of imminent use of force, and response is necessary to repel attack.

      a. **Honest & Reasonable Belief**—subjective and objective elements.

         i. **Subjective**—honest belief that there threat of force is imminent and use of responsive force necessary.

         ii. **Objective**—belief that threat of force imminent and use of responsive force necessary must be reasonable.

         iii. **Reasonable Person**—physical characteristics of accused may be considered, but not mental, emotional characteristics, or views.

      b. **Necessity & Imminency**—threat of unlawful force must be imminent and response must be necessary.

         i. **Relationship Between Elements**—imminency is one way to establish necessity; where no imminent danger, not necessary to act and defense inapplicable.

ii. **Battered Spouse Defense**—often no defense as no perceived imminency or necessity to act.

A. **Majority**—no defense.

B. **Experts**—some jurisdictions permit introduction of syndrome evidence: cycle of violence creates "learned helplessness."

c. **Aggressors**—not entitled to self defense.

i. **Test**—someone who threatens or initiates unlawful use of force.

ii. **Excessive Force**—if victim responds with excessive force, aggressor regains self defense right.

d. **Unlawful Arrest**—mixed law.

i. **Common Law**—some jurisdictions retain common law rule that permits use of force to resist unlawful arrest.

ii. **MPC**—other jurisdictions follow MPC rule that no right to use force to resist unlawful arrest, unless excessive force being used.

e. **Deadly Force**—force intended or likely to cause death or serious bodily injury.

i. **Proportionality**—most jurisdictions follow MPC approach that use of deadly force okay only if threatened with deadly force.

ii. **Aggressors**—not entitled to use deadly force in self defense.

A. **Withdrawals**—aggressor regains self defense right if withdraws other than temporarily or strategically and makes withdrawal clear.

B. **Excessive Force**—if victim responds with to use of mere force with deadly force, aggressor regains self defense right.

iii. **Retreat Doctrine**—did not exist at common law.

A. **Scope**—many jurisdictions follow MPC approach that no right to use deadly force where person knows use can be avoided with complete safety by retreating.

B. **Castle Doctrine**—retreat doctrine inapplicable where person acting in own home, and sometimes place of work or beyond.

f. **Exception**—castle doctrine often inapplicable where person was initial aggressor or used force against co-habitant or co-worker.

g. **Battered Spouse**—in some jurisdictions, battered spouse does not need to retreat before using deadly force against abusing spouse.

C. **Defense of Others**—force used to defend against threat or attack on another person.

1. **Common Law**—unlike today, limited to defense of close relatives.

2. **Alter Ego Rule**—minority rule that right to act in defense of others limited by other person's right of self defense: "step into shoes" of victim.

3. **Today**—majority: defense of others okay if person reasonably believes use of force justified and necessary under circumstances.

4. **Retreat**—retreat doctrine inapplicable unless person using force and person being defended can both retreat in complete safety.

D. **Defense of Property or Habitation**—force used to defend real or personal property.

1. **Common Law**—depended on level of force used.

a. **Unlawful Force**—force could be used to protect property when reasonable belief immediately necessary.

b. **Deadly Force**—deadly force could be used only where reasonable belief necessary to prevent imminent, forcible entry into dwelling.

2. **Majority**—force can be used when reasonable belief necessary to prevent or terminate unlawful trespass or carrying away of property.

3. **Deadly Force**—deadly force can be used by a homeowner to prevent or terminate unlawful entry into dwelling when reasonable belief intruder intends to commit felony inside.

4. **Habitation**—some jurisdictions: deadly force permitted to terminate unlawful entry into person's dwelling where reasonable belief nothing less would terminate entry.

5. **Trap Guns**—not permitted.

E. **Imperfect Defenses**—mitigating defense in murder prosecution to voluntary manslaughter.

1. **Test**—accused honestly believed needed to use protective force but belief was unreasonable.

2. **Application**—not always permitted in recklessness or negligence crimes.

F. **Law Enforcement Defense**—force used to prevent crime or make an arrest.

1. **Common Law**—law enforcement officers could use reasonably necessary force to prevent or arrest for felony.

   a. **Misdemeanors**—non-deadly force only.

   b. **Private Citizens**—depends on circumstances.

      i. **Assisting Police**—same rights as officers.

      ii. **Citizen's Arrest**—could only use force to arrest for felony.

2. **Majority**—depends on level of force used.

   a. **Unlawful Force**—law enforcement officers can use force to prevent crime or make arrest when reasonably necessary.

   b. **Deadly Force**—can be used only when reasonable belief substantial risk of serious danger if not used immediately.

G. **Necessity Defense**—commission of crime to prevent greater harm occurring from natural event.

1. **General Rule**—may commit crime when faced with imminent threat of serious injury and no reasonable and lawful alternative exists except commission of less serious crime to avoid threat.

2. **Recklessness or Negligence**—inapplicable to reckless or negligent crimes when person was reckless or negligent creating need to act.

3. **Homicide Excluded**—inapplicable to homicide charges.
4. **Objective Test**—was the criminal conduct reasonably necessary?
5. **Necessity vs. Duress**—necessity is response to natural events; duress is response to human threats.

H. **Consent of Victim**—valid defense only for some crimes.

ILLUSTRATIVE PROBLEMS

The following problems illustrate how the checklist points help to resolve questions relating to justification defenses.

■ PROBLEM 14.1 ■

Oliver Hudson was furious at Ed Belton because Belton had just broken up with Hudson's brother, Stefan, and Stefan was distraught. Hudson drove to Belton's apartment, rang the doorbell, and when Belton answered the door, Hudson pushed him to the floor and jumped on top of him, pummeling him with his fists. After a minute or so, Belton managed to break free from Hudson's attack, ran into his bedroom, and retrieved a knife from a bedside drawer. Belton then ran out of the bedroom and took off after Hudson with the knife drawn.

Meanwhile, while Belton was in the bedroom, Hudson left the apartment and took the stairs down to the parking lot. As Hudson reached his car, preparing to leave, Belton emerged from the apartment building, ran toward him, cursing and shrieking and waving his knife in the air. Hudson quickly tried to get his car started and to get out of there. But because his car window was down part of the way, Belton managed to reach the car and snake his hand through the crack in the window before Hudson could drive away. Belton managed to stab Hudson in his left shoulder.

Screaming with pain, Hudson grabbed for the glove compartment, reached inside, and removed a pistol. Meanwhile, Belton had pulled the knife blade out of Hudson's shoulder and was swinging his arm back in through the window, trying to stab Hudson again. In response, Hudson calmly aimed the pistol at Belton, pulled the trigger, and shot him.

Belton was badly injured but survived after a long convalescence. Hudson was charged with attempted murder. Can Hudson successfully defend himself against that charge by establishing self defense?

Analysis

Yes.

There is no question but that Hudson was the initial aggressor in this hypothetical. He initiated the unlawful use of force against Belton. As a result, Belton was privileged to respond to Hudson's use of force against him by using unlawful force responsively against Hudson, as necessary to defend himself. Belton also had no obligation to retreat from Hudson—even in a jurisdiction recognizing the retreat doctrine—as he was in his own dwelling when all of this occurred.

But, instead of responding to Hudson's aggression with unlawful force, Belton responded by using deadly force when he retrieved his knife and went after Hudson with it. Deadly force is the use of force that is intended or likely to cause death or serious bodily injury. The use of a knife here was clearly deadly force.

Once Hudson, who had withdrawn from the fray, was faced with Belton who was threatening to use deadly force against him, Hudson—the initial aggressor—regained his self defense right. Having regained this right, could Hudson use deadly force himself—the pistol—in shooting Belton?

To use unlawful force in self defense, Hudson needed to reasonably believe both that there was a threat of the imminent use of force against him, and that a forcible response was necessary in order to repel that attack. These elements were clearly met here. Not only was the use of force against Hudson imminent, it was already in progress. Moreover, there was no reason to believe that Belton—who was poised to strike again—would desist without Hudson's intervention.

But was Hudson privileged to use *deadly* force in responding to Belton's attack? Again, the answer is in the affirmative. Hudson was responding with deadly force to Belton's attack on him with deadly force.

As a result, Hudson can successfully defend himself against the charge of attempted murder on the basis of self defense.

■ PROBLEM 14.2 ■

Dan Zell was walking home one evening when he heard yelling and screaming coming from a nearby alley. He glanced down the alleyway entrance and saw two men, Howard Ramos and Manuel Mendez, fighting with a young woman, Ellen Dahl, who was screaming and trying to break away from them. Zell pulled out his mobile phone and yelled out: "Get away from her right now! I'm calling the police." Ramos yelled back to Zell: "Stay back. We're police officers!"

Zell did not believe Ramos, and he immediately called 911 and reported the incident. He then ran over and dragged both men off of Dahl. Dahl immediately jumped up off the ground and ran away. When Mendez tried to run after her, Zell stopped him and pushed him against the alley wall. As Mendez's head smacked against the wall, it hit at a funny angle and led to injuries that resulted ultimately in Mendez's death.

As it turned out, Ramos and Mendez were in fact both undercover police officers who had been trying to arrest Dahl for numerous sales of heroin and crack cocaine. Zell has been charged with the murder of Mendez.

What defenses, if any, does he have to this charge?

Analysis

In the first instance, Zell might well try and negative one or more of the elements of murder, raising in particular the question whether or not he actually acted with malice when he killed Mendez, *see* Chapter 12 (Homicide), and whether his push of Mendez into the wall was the legal cause of Mendez's death, *see* Chapter 5 (Causation).

But there are two affirmative defenses that he can raise on these facts as well, a complete defense and a mitigating defense.

First, he would surely raise a defense-of-others defense. If the jurisdiction in which this hypothetical took place, uses the alter ego rule, then this defense is likely to fail. Dahl did not have the right to use self defense against Ramos and Mendez who were lawfully arresting her and—as law enforcement officers—could use reasonably necessary force to do so. Presumably, they were not using excessive force in making this arrest as they were simply using their bare hands to try and restrain her. Since, under the alter ego rule, Zell stands in the shoes of Dahl and Dahl had no right to use force against Ramos and Mendez, Zell had no right to use force against them either.

In a majority jurisdiction, however, Zell would have to establish not that Dahl had the right to self defense as under the alter ego rule, but rather that he reasonably believed that the use of force was justified and necessary under these circumstances to protect Dahl from the unlawful use of force against her by Ramos and Mendez. There is no reason not to believe that Zell truly believed that he needed to act to help an innocent victim, but was this a reasonable thing to believe after Ramos yelled at him that they were police officers? How a jury answers that objective question will determine whether or not Zell can make a complete defense of defense of others to the murder charge and stand a chance of being acquitted.

Moreover, there is a second possible defense here in a majority jurisdiction that accepts imperfect defenses. Zell can make a mitigating imperfect defense in these circumstances. Zell honestly believed that he needed to use force in defense of Dahl, as discussed above. If this belief was unreasonable and, hence, not a complete defense, it would nonetheless mitigate murder to voluntary manslaughter as an imperfect defense.

■ PROBLEM 14.3 ■

Odin Knutsen grabbed Anna Maria Sprouse's purse from her and ran away as fast as he could. To his shock and surprise, however, Sprouse pulled a small pistol out of her suit jacket pocket and fired at him three times as he was running away, missing each time.

After Knutsen had run away from—and out of sight of—Sprouse and her unexpected gunfire, he then began to break into Elton Ashe's home, simply trying to find a quiet spot to take whatever was valuable out of the purse he had stolen from Sprouse. Unfortunately for Knutsen, however, he picked the wrong home to break into. The homeowner, Ashe, heard him break in the front door, ran to get their shotgun, and returned and shot Knutsen in the chest as he was still entering the house, killing him instantly.

Sprouse has been charged with attempted murder. Ashe has been charged with murder.

What defenses, if any, do each of these individuals have to these charges?

Analysis

In the first instance, Sprouse might well try and negative one or more of the elements of attempted murder, raising in particular the question whether or not she acted with the specific intent to kill when she shot at (or simply in the direction of?) Knutsen. *See* Chapter 7 (Attempt) & Chapter 12 (Homicide). Similarly, Ashe might well try and negative one or more of the elements of murder, although it is rather unlikely that they would have any success at all in taking this particular defensive approach.

But there is an affirmative defense that both Sprouse and Ashe will likely raise as well, albeit with quite different prospects of success: defense of property or habitation. Sprouse will likely argue that she had the right to re-take her stolen purse with the use of force. And that is in fact correct, except—significantly—that she did not have the right to use deadly force for this purpose, which is exactly what she did when she fired at Knutsen with her pistol. Accordingly, this affirmative defense will fail for Sprouse.

As to Ashe, the key question is what type of rule does the jurisdiction in which these events took place use for defense of habitation? In a majority of jurisdictions, the use of deadly force by a homeowner like Ashe is lawful, but only when it is used to prevent an unlawful entry into that person's dwelling when the homeowner reasonably believes that the intruder intends to commit a felony inside the home. In this case, there is no indication that Ashe had any sense at all of Knutsen's intentions when he entered Ashe's home. Accordingly, in a jurisdiction of this type, Ashe's use of deadly force would likely be deemed to have been unjustified and impermissible.

But in a more permissive, minority jurisdiction, one that also permits the use of deadly force when there has been an unlawful entry into a person's dwelling and a homeowner reasonably believes that nothing less than deadly force would be adequate to terminate that entry, Ashe's actions may well be found to be reasonable and justified. In such a jurisdiction, Ashe's belief about Knutsen's intent would be irrelevant; what would be relevant is the reasonableness of Ashe's belief that their use of deadly force was necessary to terminate Knutsen's entry. And that question, of course, is one for a jury to decide. There is every chance, however, that Ashe might be able to defend successfully against a murder charge on this basis in a jurisdiction of this sort.

■ PROBLEM 14.4 ■

Susan Sealey believes that abortion and the use of any contraception by individuals engaging in sexual intercourse is immoral and equivalent to an act of murder. To demonstrate her opposition to abortion and the use of contraceptives, she broke into a closed pharmacy late one evening, and destroyed mifepristone (an abortion pill) and all of the contraceptive agents she could find, including hundreds of condoms, intrauterine devices (IUDs), packages of birth control pills, and contraceptive foams.

Sealey was caught and prosecuted for burglary. Her defense counsel has raised a necessity defense on her behalf.

Can Sealey defend herself successfully using a necessity defense?

Analysis

No.

A necessity defense is available in a majority of jurisdictions only when a person is faced with an imminent threat of serious injury and has no reasonable, lawful alternative other than to commit a less serious crime in order to avoid that threat. Sealey honestly believes that contraceptives pose a threat of serious injury. But the necessity defense does not turn upon the accused person's subjective beliefs about whether it was necessary to avoid a greater evil. Rather, the test is an objective one, i.e. whether there was in fact a greater evil to be avoided. Whatever Sealey believes, the use of contraceptive devices is not unlawful and not deemed to be a homicidal act. Accordingly, with respect to this element alone, Sealey's necessity defense will clearly fail.

Moreover, Sealey would also not be able to satisfy the imminence element of the necessity defense. She could not establish that a threat of serious injury was imminent at the time that she acted.

Nor was her commission of a criminal act—burglary—the only reasonable alternative she had to demonstrate her personal moral opposition to the use of contraceptives. She could have engaged in any number of lawful acts of protest, for example.

Indeed, Sealey's actions were acts of civil disobedience. People who knowingly violate the criminal law to demonstrate their moral, ideological, religious or political sentiments should expect that they will have to face the punishment that the criminal law imposes as a result of their knowing violation of those laws.

POINTS TO REMEMBER

- Justification defenses involve external issues; excuse defenses involve internal issues.
- Non-aggressor may use force in self defense when reasonable belief threat of imminent use of force exists and response is necessary to repel attack.
- For self defense, belief that threat is imminent and response necessary must be both honest and reasonable.
- For self defense, threat must be in fact imminent and response must be necessary.
- No battered spouse self defense right where neither imminency nor necessity to act, but expert testimony sometimes possible about battered spouse syndrome.

- Aggressors not entitled to self defense unless victim responds with excessive force.
- Deadly force may be used in self defense only if person using it threatened with deadly force.
- Majority holds no right to deadly force if it can be avoided with complete safety by retreating.
- Retreat before use of deadly force inapplicable in one's own home or office unless response to co-habitant or co-worker.
- Use of non-deadly force to protect property lawful where reasonable belief immediately necessary.
- Use of deadly force okay where reasonable belief necessary to prevent imminent entry into dwelling and (majority:) intruder intends to commit felony.
- Police can use force to prevent crimes or make arrests when reasonably necessary.
- Police can use deadly force only when they reasonably believe substantial risk of serious and immediate danger.
- Necessity defense available when imminent threat of serious injury and no alternative exists except commission of less serious crime.
- Necessity defense inapplicable both to conditions created by person using it, and to homicides.

CHAPTER 15

Excuses

Excuses are criminal law defenses that are accepted because the person acting is deemed not to be blameworthy for some appropriate reason. Justification defenses *see* Chapter 14 (Justification Defenses), in contrast, are criminal law defenses permitted in order to allow a person to make an appropriate response to certain external events. Or you can simply look at this distinction this way:

- excuses = internal issues;
- justification defenses = external issues.

Affirmative defenses. Excuses are often made "affirmative defenses" by statute. An affirmative defense does not depend upon defense counsel negativing (by creating a reasonable doubt as to) one of the elements of a crime. Instead, even if all of those elements have been proved, a defendant may defend affirmatively by proving the separate elements of an affirmative defense set out by statute.

Ordinarily, the burden of proof on a defendant for making an affirmative defense is proof by a preponderance of the evidence.

A. DURESS

In general. Duress is a defense when a crime is committed by a person only because that person reasonably believed that he or she was being coerced by another person into committing that crime as a result of an unlawful and imminent threat of death or serious bodily harm to the person being coerced or to a third party. "A person who acts under duress is not morally blameworthy—that is part of what it means to say that duress excuses otherwise-criminal conduct." *Ruan v. United States*, 142 S. Ct. 2370, 2382, 2386 (2022) (Alito, J. conc'g).

Nature of threat. The unlawful threat supporting a duress defense must be a threat that a reasonable person could not be expected to resist, e.g. actions undertaken at gunpoint. This threat is measured by an objective test which focuses upon the actual coercion used, rather than a subjective test that would turn on the amount of coercion that the person believed (perhaps erroneously) that he or she was facing.

A minority of jurisdictions limit the permissible coercive threats that may support a duress defense, however, to threats to the person actually acting or to a defined class of close relatives (rather than to any third party).

Model Penal Code. Model Penal Code (MPC) § 2.09(1) provides that "[i]t is an affirmative defense that the actor engaged in the conduct charged to constitute an offense because he was coerced to do so by the use of, or a threat to use, unlawful force against his person or the person of another, which a person of reasonable firmness in his situation would have been unable to resist."

Reckless or negligent conduct. MPC § 2.09(2) excludes use of a duress defense, however, when the person acting "recklessly placed himself in a situation in which it was probable that he would be subjected to duress." And "[t]he defense is also unavailable if he was negligent in placing himself in such a situation, whenever negligence suffices to establish culpability for the offense charged."

This limitation on the duress defense is widely followed. A person may not create the conditions that lead to a duress defense and then use that defense.

Homicide excluded. Most jurisdictions do not permit use of a duress defense to excuse a person's commission of a homicide crime.

Prison escapes. A duress defense is often attempted when a person is charged with escaping from a correctional institution. In some jurisdictions, in this setting, an additional element must be proved to make this defense successfully, namely that the escapee made a good faith effort to turn himself or herself in to authorities after escaping the coercive force that created the duress.

Duress vs. necessity. Duress is an excuse, relating to a response to human threats; necessity is a justification defense, *see* Chapter 14 (Justification Defenses), relating to a response to threats from natural events.

B. INTOXICATION & DRUGGED CONDITION

A potential defense based upon the fact that a person was intoxicated or in a drugged condition at the time that he or she committed a crime, thus negativing the requisite mens rea, is discussed elsewhere in this volume. *See* Chapter 3 (Mens Rea).

C. PSYCHOLOGICAL DEFENSES

The U.S. Constitution does not require that a jurisdiction take any specific approach to the question when, if ever, an accused person should be relieved of criminal responsibility because of his or her mental disease or psychological condition. *Clark v. Arizona*, 548 U.S. 735, 753 (2006) ("the insanity rule, like the conceptualization of criminal offenses, is substantially open to state choice").

As the Supreme Court has explained: "Defining the precise relationship between criminal culpability and mental illness involves examining the workings of the brain, the purposes of the criminal law, the ideas of free will and responsibility. It is a project demanding hard choices among values, in a context replete with uncertainty, even at a single moment in time. And it is a project, if any is, that should be open to revision over time, as new medical knowledge emerges and as legal and moral norms evolve. Which is all to say that it is a project for state governance, not constitutional law. . . . No insanity rule in this country's heritage or history was ever so settled as to tie a State's hands centuries later." *Kahler v. Kansas*, 140 S. Ct. 1021, 1037 (2020).

As a result, the federal government and the states vary widely in the approaches that they have adopted to deal with the issue of an individual's responsibility for criminal acts committed while he or she was suffering from some form of mental impairment.

1. Insanity

Most (but not all) jurisdictions recognize a defense of insanity. A person found to be not guilty by reason of insanity (NGRI) is excused completely from any criminal responsibility for the crimes with which he or she has been charged.

An accused person found to be insane is thereby found to be not guilty and is discharged from the criminal justice system. Nonetheless, he or she usually faces civil commitment proceedings immediately subsequent to the NGRI verdict, assuming—as is typical—that his or her mental illness is continuing and that he or she poses a threat to self or to others.

Focus on time crime committed. An insanity defense focuses only upon the accused person's mental state at the time that the crime charged was committed.

The insanity inquiry is therefore unrelated to the separate question of the accused person's subsequent "competency" to stand trial. Competency is measured by the accused person's ability at that time to understand the nature or object of the proceedings and to participate and assist in his or her defense.

Different tests. Jurisdictions use a variety of different tests to determine whether a person was insane at the time that he or she committed the crime in question.

The Supreme Court found in 2006 that "[s]eventeen States and the Federal Government have adopted a recognizable version of the *M'Naghten* test [*see below*] with both its cognitive incapacity and moral incapacity components. One State has adopted only *M'Naghten's* cognitive incapacity test, and 10 . . . have adopted the moral incapacity test alone. Fourteen jurisdictions, inspired by the Model Penal Code, have in place an amalgam of the volitional incapacity test and some variant of the moral incapacity test. . . Three States combine a full *M'Naghten* test with a volitional incapacity formula. And New Hampshire alone stands by the product-of-mental-illness test." *Clark v. Arizona*, 548 U.S. 735, 750–51 (2006). *See also Kahler v. Kansas*, 140 S. Ct. 1021, 1037 (2020) (Appendix, listing states' tests as of 2020).

Expert testimony. Both the prosecution and the defense often use the testimony of psychological or psychiatric experts to help the jury determine whether or not an accused person was so mentally ill at the time that he or she committed a crime that he or she should be found to be insane and, hence, NGRI.

Legal vs. medical point of view. It is important to note that the term "insanity" is a legal term of art; it is not a psychological or psychiatric concept.

Insanity describes that specific mental condition that a particular jurisdiction has concluded should and does absolve someone from responsibility for their criminal acts. As a result, a person may well have a serious mental disorder (in a psychologist's or a psychiatrist's medical view), and yet not be insane within the legal meaning of that term. In fact, this is a very common occurrence.

a. M'Naghten *Test*

The English test for insanity is called the "*M'Naghten* test": "A person is not responsible for criminal conduct if at the time of such conduct he was suffering from such a mental disease or defect as not to know the nature and quality of the act or, if he did know, that he did not know that what he was doing was wrong."

This test was first announced in *Daniel M'Naghten's Case*, 10 Cl. & F. 200, 8 Eng. Rep. 718 (House of Lords 1843). After it was adopted by the House of Lords, it quickly became the most common insanity test used in American jurisdictions as well.

As the Supreme Court noted above, the *M'Naghten* test (or versions of it) is still the most common form of insanity test used in the United States. The classic test has two prongs, but a jurisdiction using *M'naghten* need not use both of these prongs. *See Kahler v. Kansas*, 140 S. Ct. 1021, 1037 (2020) ("it is not for the courts to insist on any single criterion going forward").

i. Cognitive Incapacity Prong

The cognitive incapacity prong of the *M'Naghten* test asks whether "at the time of [the criminal] conduct[, the accused] was suffering from such a mental disease or defect as not to know the nature and quality of the act."

The focus of this part of the *M'Naghten* test is on the question whether a mental defect left the accused unable to understand what he or she was doing.

ii. Moral Incapacity Prong

The moral incapacity prong of the *M'Naghten* test asks whether, at the time of the criminal conduct in question, the accused "did not know that what he was doing was wrong."

The focus of this part of the *M'Naghten* test is on the question whether a mental disease or defect left the accused unable to understand that his or her actions were wrong.

iii. Irresistible Impulse Test

Some jurisdictions also use an "irresistible impulse" test. In these jurisdictions, even if the cognitive and moral incapacity prongs of the *M'Naghten* test are not satisfied, an accused person is nonetheless deemed to be insane if he or she is found to have acted pursuant to an irresistible and uncontrollable impulse stemming from mental disease that rendered him or her powerless to resist.

b. Product-of-Mental Illness Test

In 1954, the D.C. Circuit Court of Appeals adopted an insanity test that provided basically that an accused person was insane if his or her criminal act was the "product of mental disease or mental defect." *Durham v. United States*, 94 U.S.App.D.C. 228, 214 F.2d 862 (1954).

This test was designed to defer to perceived advances in psychiatric knowledge. Often called the "*Durham* test," only New Hampshire uses a variant of this test today.

c. *ALI Model Penal Code Test*

MPC § 4.01(1) provides that "[a] person is not responsible for criminal conduct if at the time of such conduct as a result of mental disease or defect he lacks substantial capacity either to appreciate the wrongfulness of his conduct or to conform his conduct to the requirements of law."

MPC § 4.01(2) further provides that "the terms 'mental disease or defect' do not include an abnormality manifested only by repeated criminal or otherwise anti-social conduct."

The American Law Institute's (ALI) MPC insanity test (often called simply the "ALI test") expanded the scope of mental impairment that sufficed to establish insanity over the more limited *M'Naghten* test. It was the majority test used in the United States until the trial of John Hinckley for the attempted assassination of President Ronald Reagan.

After Hinckley's NGRI verdict in his 1981 trial, many jurisdictions reconsidered their approach to insanity, and subsequently dropped the MPC test, most often returning to a version of the *M'Naghten* test.

2. Guilty but Mentally Ill

Some jurisdictions also recognize a defense of "guilty but mentally ill" (GBMI). In those jurisdictions, an accused person who raises an insanity defense but is found *not* to have been insane at the time of the commission of the crime can nonetheless be found by the jury to be GBMI under a broader and more inclusive definition of "mental illness."

Additionally, with the permission of the prosecution, a person can simply plead GBMI, similar to offering a guilty plea.

Consequences of GBMI verdict. An accused person found to be insane is discharged from the criminal justice system altogether, although he or she usually faces civil commitment proceedings after the NGRI verdict if his or her mental illness is continuing and he or she poses a threat to self or others.

An accused person found to be GBMI, in contrast, is sentenced just as if he or she had been found simply to have been guilty. But a convicted GBMI offender—unlike a person acquitted as NGRI—is entitled to be treated for his or her mental illness in the criminal justice system.

After this treatment for his or her mental illness is completed, a person the convicted GBMI offender is returned to the criminal justice system, usually to complete the remaining time left on his or her original sentence.

3. Diminished Capacity

Some jurisdictions further recognize a "diminished capacity" (sometimes called "diminished responsibility") defense. In these jurisdictions—California is the most prominent example—diminished capacity is usually made out when an accused person establishes in the minds of a criminal jury that he or she did not have the mental capacity necessary to possess the mens rea required for the specific crime charged.

A diminished capacity defense can also be viewed as simply a way of negativing the requisite mens rea element of a crime in these jurisdictions, *see* Chapter 3 (Mens Rea), rather than as a traditional excuse defense.

Model Penal Code. MPC § 4.02(1) provides that "[e]vidence that the defendant suffered from a mental disease or defect is admissible whenever it is relevant to prove that the defendant did or did not have a state of mind which is an element of the offense."

Complete or mitigating defense. Depending upon the jurisdiction, a finding of diminished capacity might serve as a complete defense, or it may instead be treated as a mitigating defense acting to reduce the severity of some specified crime—usually murder (to manslaughter)—with which the accused is has been charged. *See* Chapter 12 (Homicide).

Insanity distinguished. Insanity is a complete defense to any criminal charge. Diminished capacity is a way of negativing the mens rea of a specific criminal offense or mitigating its severity which usually can be made out with a lesser showing of mental disorder than is necessary to establish insanity.

D. ENTRAPMENT

A claim of entrapment can be used as a complete defense to criminal charges when an accused person establishes that his or her criminal activity was actually the product of significant government encouragement.

Subjective vs. objective test. Federal courts use a subjective entrapment test which focuses on the question whether or not the accused was predisposed to commit the crime in question. But the states are split on this issue. Some use a subjective test just like the federal courts.

Other states use an objective test. The objective entrapment defense focuses on the nature of the police conduct in encouraging or assisting the accused in committing the crime in question. In objective-test entrapment jurisdictions, the accused person's predisposition to commit the crime is irrelevant. The question is, instead: how outrageous was the police conduct?

Model Penal Code. MPC § 2.13(1) adopts the objective approach to entrapment: "A public law enforcement official or a person acting in cooperation with such an official perpetrates an entrapment if for the purpose of obtaining evidence of the commission of an offense, he induces or encourages another person to engage in conduct constituting such offense by either: (a) making knowingly false representations designed to induce the belief that such conduct is not prohibited; or (b) employing methods of persuasion or inducement which create a substantial risk that such an offense will be committed by persons other than those who are ready to commit it."

MPC § 2.13(3) provides, furthermore, that an entrapment defense is inapplicable "when causing or threatening bodily injury is an element of the offense charged and the prosecution is based on conduct causing or threatening such injury to a person other than the person perpetrating the entrapment."

Past conduct. Under the subjective approach, an accused person's character, reputation, and past criminal conduct are all relevant to the determination whether or not he or she was entrapped. In an objective jurisdiction, the accused person's character, reputation, and past conduct are irrelevant.

Opportunity to commit crime. The government's act of simply giving a person an opportunity to commit a crime is not enough, in and of itself, to make out the defense of entrapment.

Similarly, the use of an undercover agent and his or her lies and deceit in dealing with a person who is considering the commission of a crime are not enough, in and of themselves, to establish entrapment.

Violent crimes. Some jurisdictions do not permit the use of an entrapment defense to defend against commission of a violent crime. Most often, entrapment is used as a defense in so-called "victimless crime" prosecutions, like sale or possession of narcotics.

E. DE MINIMIS DEFENSE

Some jurisdictions permit a trial judge to dismiss criminal charges because the underlying conduct charged as constituting the offense is de minimis, i.e. it is deemed to be too petty or trivial to merit criminal prosecution.

Model Penal Code. MPC § 2.12 provides that a court should dismiss a prosecution if the underlying conduct "was within a customary license or tolerance," "did not actually cause or threaten the harm or evil" contemplated by the statute or "did so only to an extent too trivial" to warrant conviction, or was otherwise not within the range of conduct the legislature anticipated would be criminalized.

EXCUSES CHECKLIST

A. **In General**—excuses permitted as defenses because person's actions deemed not to be blameworthy.

   1. **Excuses vs. Justifications**—excuses = internal issues; justifications = external issues.

   2. **Affirmative Defenses**—many excuses are affirmative defenses.

      a. **Relationship to Proof of Crime**—even if elements of crime proven, defendant may use affirmative defense by proving separate exculpatory elements.

      b. **Burden of Proof**—usually preponderance of evidence not beyond a reasonable doubt.

B. **Duress**—excusable commission of crime due to coercion.

   1. **General Rule**—may commit crime where reasonable belief of coercion by another with unlawful and imminent threat of death or serious bodily harm to actor or third party.

   2. **Nature of Threat**—threat must be one reasonable person could not be expected to resist.

      a. **Objective Test**—focus on actual coercion, not coerced person's belief.

      b. **Threat to Third Parties**—majority rule; minority: only threats to close relatives.

   3. **Recklessness or Negligence**—no duress where person recklessly or negligently placed self in probable duress situation.

   4. **Homicide Excluded**—inapplicable to homicide charges.

5. **Prison Escapes**—sometimes additional requirement of good faith effort to turn self in after escape and duress ended.

6. **Duress vs. Necessity**—duress is response to human threats; necessity is response to natural events.

C. **Psychological Defenses**—no single approach required by Constitution.

1. **Insanity**—not guilty by reason of insanity (NGRI) verdict is complete defense.

    a. **Time of Crime**—insanity focus is time crime committed unlike competency focus on trial and ability to understand proceedings and participate in defense.

    b. **Post-NGRI**—discharge from criminal system but civil commitment proceedings.

    c. **Legal vs. Medical Tests**—insanity is legal term of art not medical.

    d. **Experts**—expert testimony can help jury decide if legal insanity test met.

    e. **Tests**—no one approach required and variety used.

        i. ***M'Naghten* Test**—traditional and most widely used: "A person is not responsible for criminal conduct if at the time of such conduct he was suffering from such a mental disease or defect as not to know the nature and quality of the act or, if he did know, that he did not know that what he was doing was wrong."

            A. **Cognitive Incapacity Prong**—"nature and quality" of act: focus on whether mental defect left accused unable to understand what he or she was doing.

            B. **Moral Incapacity Prong**—"did not know that what he was doing was wrong": focus on whether a mental disease or defect left accused unable to understand actions were wrong.

            C. **Irresistible Impulse**—in addition to *M'Naghten,* minority: also insane if acted on uncontrollable impulse rendering actor powerless to resist.

ii. **MPC Test**—"[a] person is not responsible for criminal conduct if at the time of such conduct as a result of mental disease or defect he lacks substantial capacity either to appreciate the wrongfulness of his conduct or to conform his conduct to the requirements of law."

A. ***M'Naghten* Distinguished**—MPC test includes more types and degree of mental impairment.

B. **Hinckley Trial**—John Hinckley NGRI verdict in 1981 resulted in many jurisdictions dropping MPC test.

2. **Guilty but Mentally Ill**—minority: GBMI possible verdict for accused persons trying to get NGRI verdict.

a. **Insanity Distinguished**—GBMI test includes more types and degree of mental impairment than insanity test.

b. **Consequences**—different from NGRI.

i. **Criminal System**—no discharge from criminal system.

ii. **Sentencing**—sentenced as if guilty verdict.

iii. **Treatment**—right to treatment for mental illness.

iv. **Post-Cure**—returned to criminal system to complete sentence after recovery.

3. **Diminished Capacity**—accused did not have mental capacity to possess mens rea required for crime charged.

a. **Insanity Distinguished**—diminished capacity only negatives mens rea of certain crimes and is established with less serious showing of mental disorder.

b. **Consequences**—complete or mitigating defense for specific crimes, depending on jurisdiction.

D. **Entrapment**—defense where crime was product of police encouragement.

1. **Subjective Approach**—was accused predisposed to commit crime?

a. **Federal Test**—federal approach and approach in some states.

   b. **Past Conduct**—character, reputation, and past criminal conduct relevant.

2. **Objective Approach**—how outrageous was the police conduct?

   a. **MPC Test**—MPC approach and approach in some states.

   b. **Past Conduct**—irrelevant.

3. **Mere Opportunity to Commit Crime**—not enough.

4. **Violent Crimes**—inapplicable.

E. **De Minimis Defense**—trivial charges may be dismissed by trial judge.

ILLUSTRATIVE PROBLEMS

The following problems illustrate how the checklist points help to resolve questions relating to excuses.

■ PROBLEM 15.1 ■

Charmaine McFalls robbed a liquor store using a fake gun in order to obtain money to feed her two hungry children. She was quickly apprehended by the police and charged with robbery. McFalls plans to use the defense of duress at trial as she honestly believed that her children might starve to death if she didn't commit this robbery.

Does this defense have a chance of success?

Analysis

No.

Duress is a good defense only when a crime is committed because the person committing it reasonably believed that he or she was being coerced by another person into committing that crime as a result of an unlawful and imminent threat of death or serious bodily harm to the person being coerced or by a third party.

In this case, a duress defense fails for a number of reasons: McFalls was not being coerced by another person; the threat to her children was neither unlawful nor imminent; and her belief in the necessity of acting in this fashion was objectively unreasonable.

The coercive threat supporting a duress defense must be one that a reasonable person could not be expected to resist. It is an element that is measured objectively, focusing in this situation on the actual threat McFalls faced, rather than a subjective test that turns on the threat that McFalls believed that she was facing. While McFalls may have honestly believed that breaking the law was the only avenue open to her to keep her children from starving, such a belief would likely be viewed as unreasonable. This is so given the likely availability of social service or private, charitable relief available to people in McFalls' situation.

Parenthetically, had McFalls attempted to make a necessity defense, *see* Chapter 14 (Justification Defenses), instead of a duress defense, she would have had no greater chance of success. A necessity defense is available when a person commits a crime when faced with an imminent threat of serious injury and there is no reasonable and lawful alternative available to that person except commission of a less serious crime in order to avoid that threat. In this case, an imminent threat of starvation did not exist and, as just discussed, other reasonable and lawful alternatives existed for McFalls to pursue before she committed the crime of robbery.

■ PROBLEM 15.2 ■

Eliza Halverson, who has a mental disorder, heard a rattling noise at her front door and thought that someone was trying to break into her home. This took place during the Covid-19 Pandemic, and Halverson believed (falsely) that anyone entering her residence would invariably spread that disease to her and kill her. In fact, the noise was simply caused by a uniformed delivery person for a package delivery service, Bob Franklin. Franklin had just left a package on Halverson's doorstep.

Halverson ran to the door, saw Franklin walking away from her home on his way back to his truck, pulled her gun out of her bathrobe pocket, and shot and killed him.

Halverson has been charged with murder. Her lawyer plans to use an insanity defense on her behalf. What chance of success does Halverson have in being found not guilty by reason of insanity?

Analysis

Her chances of success depend both on the test for insanity used in this jurisdiction (assuming that this jurisdiction recognizes an insanity defense), and the fact-finding of the jury.

If this jurisdiction uses both prongs of the *M'Naghten* test, Halverson's attorney would have to prove that she was suffering from such a mental disease or defect as not to know the nature and quality of the act she committed or, if she did know, that she did not know that what she was doing was wrong.

As to the "nature and quality of her act"—the cognitive prong of *M'Naghten*—Halverson did not meet this test. She understood clearly that she was aiming her gun at Franklin and was shooting at him. In a jurisdiction that uses only this *M'Naghten* prong as its complete insanity test, Halverson's insanity defense would surely fail.

With respect to the second, moral incapacity, prong of *M'Naghten*—that she "did not know that what she was doing was wrong"—a jury could reasonably decide this issue either way. Most likely, a jury would find that Halverson was well aware that shooting another person was wrong, but that she thought—incorrectly, of course—that she was justified in these circumstances in acting for self-protective reasons. (*See* discussion of imperfect defenses below.) If the jury reasoned in that fashion, Halverson's insanity defense under *M'Naghten* would fail as neither prong of *M'Naghten* would have been met.

But it is also possible—if perhaps less likely—that a jury might find that Halverson's mental disorder was so severe that she did not even realize that shooting someone was wrong. It would be unlikely for a jury to reach a conclusion of this sort unless the jurors had heard and relied upon expert testimony presented by the defense to that effect. But the use of such expert testimony in insanity-defense cases is common. If the jury did reach this conclusion and this jurisdiction used only the second—moral incapacity—prong of *M'Naghten* or used both prongs as its insanity test, Halverson's insanity defense would succeed.

There is no evidence in these hypothetical facts to suggest that Halverson was acting in response to an irresistible impulse, which would be relevant if this jurisdiction was one of the few that has adopted that supplementary test to *M'Naghten*.

If this jurisdiction uses the MPC's insanity test instead of *M'Naghten*, Halverson's attorney would have to prove that at the time of this shooting, as a result of her mental disease or defect, Halverson lacked substantial capacity either to appreciate the wrongfulness of her conduct or to conform her conduct to the requirements of the law. In this case, as with the moral incapacity prong of the *M'Naghten* test and for much the same reasons discussed above, a jury could reasonably decide this issue either way. Here, too, the opinions of psychological or psychiatric experts testifying for the defense and the prosecution are likely to be extremely useful and persuasive to a jury in reaching a conclusion on this score.

Parenthetically, as noted above, Halverson might also raise a mitigating imperfect defense of self defense or defense of her habitation. *See* Chapter 14 (Justification Defenses). An imperfect defense is a traditional protective defense where the accused honestly believed that he or she needed to use deadly force in order to take protective action, but that belief was unreasonable. *See* Chapter 12 (Homicide). This defense would be unlikely to succeed on these facts, however, as there is no evidence that Halverson believed that she actually *needed* to use deadly force in these circumstances.

■ PROBLEM 15.3 ■

Sarah Drinkwater had previously been convicted of either possession of marijuana with intent to deliver or sale of marijuana on four prior occasions. Officer Dan Schneider was aware of Drinkwater's criminal history and, posing undercover as an unkempt graduate student, he approached Drinkwater and asked her if she would sell him some "weed." Drinkwater told Schneider to "go away," but when he persisted, she told him to try and talk to her friend, Amelia Scott, who lived in an apartment two doors down the hall and that "maybe she would have something" to sell him.

Schneider went to Scott's apartment and told her that Drinkwater had told him that Scott had some of Drinkwater's marijuana (not true) and that Drinkwater had told him to tell Scott to give it to him (also not true). Scott seemed confused about all of this (understandably, as it was not true). She told Schneider that she didn't have any of Drinkwater's marijuana, but since he was apparently such a good friend of hers, she would sell him an ounce of her own "weed" at a discount price, $200. (That was actually the normal cost of an ounce of marijuana at that time in that place.) Schneider bought the ounce.

He then returned to Drinkwater's apartment and told her that he had just seen Scott and that she had said that he should ask Drinkwater to sell him some of the "weed" she was keeping for Scott (another lie, of course). Schneider added that he would pay her $1,000 for an ounce of marijuana as he had plenty of money to spend and he didn't care about the cost. Drinkwater sold him an ounce of marijuana for $1,000.

Drinkwater and Scott were both arrested and charged with sale of marijuana in a jurisdiction still criminalizing that offense. They both plan to use an entrapment defense.

What are their chances of success in using that defense?

Analysis

Not very good.

As to Drinkwater, if the jurisdiction uses a subjective entrapment defense, she has virtually no chance of success at all. In a subjective jurisdiction, there is no entrapment if the accused was predisposed to commit the crime in question. In assessing predisposition, the jury may consider her character, reputation, and past criminal conduct. Drinkwater has a long record of marijuana offenses. The heavy likelihood, accordingly, is that she would be found to have been predisposed to commit this crime. As a result, an entrapment defense would not succeed in a subjective jurisdiction.

In an objective jurisdiction, the question instead is just how outrageous was the police conduct? Merely providing Drinkwater with an opportunity to commit this crime through use of deceit by an undercover agent is not enough to establish entrapment in either a subjective or an objective jurisdiction. In this case, the only real argument that Drinkwater can make relating to outrageous police conduct is the very high and excessive price that Schneider paid her for the marijuana. Was that conduct outrageous? A reasonable jury could decide that issue either way. As a result, depending on resolution of that factual question, an entrapment defense might or might not succeed for Drinkwater in an objective entrapment jurisdiction.

As to Scott, however, there is virtually no chance of making an entrapment defense successfully. Once again, merely providing a person with an opportunity to commit a crime, even when it is made available through the use of deceit by an undercover agent, is not enough to establish entrapment under either a subjective or objective analysis. And Scott, unlike Drinkwater, cannot claim that the government overreached by offering her an excessive amount of money to commit this crime. Schneider paid the going rate. As a result, an entrapment defense made on Scott's behalf will fail.

POINTS TO REMEMBER

- Justification defenses involve external issues; excuse defenses involve internal issues.
- Duress defense is available where reasonable belief of coercion by another with unlawful, imminent threat of death or serious bodily harm to person or third party.
- Duress threat must be one reasonable person could not be expected to resist.

- Duress defense inapplicable to homicides and where recklessly or negligently put self in probable duress situation.

  Insanity defense and particular insanity test not required.

- Insanity focus is time of crime; competency focus is time of trial.
- Most common insanity test is *M'Naghten* focused on nature and quality of act and whether actor knew wrongfulness of conduct.
- In a few states, accused seeking NGRI can be found GBMI instead on lesser showing of mental disorder.
- Where diminished capacity defense recognized, accused can show did not have mental capacity to possess mens rea required for crime charged.
- Entrapment subjective approach (some jurisdictions): was accused predisposed to commit crime?
- Entrapment objective approach (some jurisdictions): how outrageous was the police conduct?
- Defendant's character, reputation, and past criminal conduct relevant only to subjective entrapment approach.
- Mere opportunity to commit crime is not enough to establish entrapment.

Conclusion: General Examination Tips

Now that you have had a chance to look at the full set of checklists for each of the specific topics that you have covered or will be covering in criminal law, please consider some nuggets of general advice to help you ace your criminal law examination:

Before the Examination

- Prepare early for examinations by reviewing information learned as you go along rather than waiting until the end of the semester.
- Review the material you have learned by applying it to hypothetical problems. (Maybe your professor or your law school has some old exams available for you to look at and use for practice purposes.) It is important to gain experience answering and actually writing out answers to problems well before the exam season begins.
- Meet with your professor regularly to gain useful insight into what he or she feels is important about particular topics and to develop a deeper understanding of the material. This time can also be used to obtain information regarding the type of analysis the professor expects to see from students on an examination.
- Synthesize the material by recognizing the connections between different topics covered within the course to develop a more comprehensive view of the material.
- Do not neglect information regarding the basic policy underpinnings or implications of various legal principles learned in the course. These policies often are important in equipping you with the ability to resolve tough questions at the margins of the law, and they provide you with the rationales you need to have at hand to explain particular legal outcomes.
- Do not rely on mere mastery of the substantive rules and doctrines to prepare for the exam. What is equally important is a deep *understanding* of this material which will enable you to engage in high-level analysis of the problems that you will face on the exam.

During the Examination

- Before writing a response to a question, be sure that you understand precisely what the professor is asking you to do, e.g., giving the arguments on both sides of an issue or on behalf of only one party, assuming the role of the judge writing an opinion in the case, etc. Briefly outline your answer before writing in order to facilitate your ability to provide a clear, organized response and to structure your thinking about the question to ensure that your answer covers all of the issues that need to be addressed.
- On the exam, law professors are not simply looking for students to apply the law they have been taught to a given set of facts to achieve a result. In addition to demonstrating that ability, superior exam takers also demonstrate a depth of understanding that goes beyond their mere recognition of and facility with the black-letter law rules. The recognition of what lies behind difficult questions and reference to underlying policies is the mark of a good answer.
- Always identify your assumptions. If you are assuming certain facts as the basis for your answer, make those assumptions explicit. But don't assume away the difficult issues that your professor wants you to address.
- Unless the question asks for a very brief answer, never give a simple conclusion regarding the proper result as your only answer on an exam. Provide a full explanation showing (and showing off) your analysis. Remember this: showing how you reached your conclusion is much more important than the conclusion itself.
- Rather than simply reaching a particular result because a certain case calls for that result, reason toward a conclusion by identifying key facts in the question, similar facts in other relevant cases, and any policy issues that support the outcome you intend to reach.
- Regardless of how difficult the question may seem, an answer to an examination question must reach a result. Do not equivocate, unless a factual ambiguity invites you to explore alternative analytical paths. In that case, explain and address that ambiguity. Where you can, use legal judgment, reasoning, and analysis to identify the best answer available and provide arguments supporting your choice.
- Consider the arguments on both sides of an issue and state them. Then take the opportunity to apply your understanding of

the principles and policies involved as well as any relevant precedent to reach a particular result.

- When deciding between two competing approaches to resolving an issue, clearly state which approach you intend to apply and articulate the arguments for why that is the better approach.
- First-year law school exams are often competitive affairs in the sense that one's performance is evaluated against the performance of other students. As a result, simply knowing the material and properly applying the law to the facts may not be enough for you to excel where your peers can do the same thing. *Show off!* Distinguish yourself where there is time to do it by engaging in an analysis that demonstrates your depth of knowledge and a true understanding rather than rote memorization or dexterity with available source material (for open-book exams).
- Oh, don't forget. In addition to the quality of your answer, make sure that you provide an answer that identifies and addresses *all* of the issues raised in the question. Applying legal rules to hypothetical examples is a very good way to develop and hone the ability to spot issues, making it critical that you work with practice questions prior to the exam.

After the Examination

It's over. Don't waste time talking with your classmates about the exam. You'll just create more unnecessary anxiety for yourself. Focus on the next exam; or, if criminal law is your last exam, celebrate being done. *Hopefully, you aced it!*

APPENDIX

Mini-Checklists

NATURE OF CRIMINAL LAW

A. **The Basics**—the criminal law was but is no longer based upon the English Common Law.

1. **Statutes**—every jurisdiction has its own criminal statutes defining the elements of crimes.
2. **Codes**—some jurisdictions have Crimes Codes and some (e.g. federal) do not.
3. **Classification of Crimes**—felonies are more serious crimes than misdemeanors.
4. **Model Penal Code**—many provisions adopted in Crimes Codes and referenced in court decisions.
5. **Proving Crimes**—each element of a crime must be proved by the prosecution beyond a reasonable doubt.

B. **Justifications for Punishment**—often used to determine what activity is criminalized and, if so, how severe the punishment can or will be.

1. **General Deterrence**—criminal punishments deter *other* people from committing that act.
2. **Specific Deterrence**—criminal punishment deters the actor from committing that act again.
3. **Incapacitation**—incarceration keeps people from committing crimes.
4. **Rehabilitation**—people can be "cured" of their criminal tendencies.
5. **Retribution**—just deserts and vengeance justify criminal punishment.
6. **Expression of Community Values**—criminal punishment educates people about what is wrong.

C. **Capital Punishment**—the Supreme Court has held the death penalty constitutional on the basis of retribution and general deterrence and not "cruel and unusual," but some states still don't use it.

ACTUS REUS

A. **The Basics**—all criminal offenses contain one or more act requirements.

1. **Actus Reus**—traditional name for act requirement ("scienter").

2. **Thought Crimes**—do not exist; there must be actus reus.

3. **Statutes**—actus reus is usually set out in criminal statute.

B. **Voluntary Act**—actus reus of criminal offense must be committed voluntarily.

1. **Involuntary Act Defense**—if accused acted involuntarily, actus reus element is not established and no crime.

2. **Involuntariness Definition**—act is involuntary if it is *not* a product of person's free will, manifested by corresponding, external body movement.

3. **Examples**—sleepwalking, actions while unconscious, reflexes.

4. **Mens Rea Irrelevant**—involuntariness is defense whether or not accused possessed mens rea and whether or not crime is strict liability.

C. **Possession**—some crimes have actus reus requiring proof of possession of something.

1. **Possession Defined**—awareness of possession to degree sufficient to be able to exercise control, while acting knowingly and voluntarily.

2. **Joint Possession**—possession by more than one person simultaneously when item found in place where more than one person was aware of existence and exercised control over it.

3. **Constructive Possession**—possession of contraband when found not on or around accused, but in place where person was aware of existence and exercised control over it.

D. **Status-Based Crimes**—person cannot be convicted merely for "status," e.g. as a narcotics addict.

1. **Rationale**—status may be acquired as result of disease, or otherwise innocently or involuntarily without fault on part of accused.
2. **Status vs. Act**—person can be convicted for committing criminal offense based upon act that was result of status, e.g. public drunkenness.

E. **Omissions**—accused cannot ordinarily be convicted of crime based upon failure to act.

1. **Exceptions: Duty-to-Aid**—minority jurisdictions require people to assist victims being harmed.
2. **Exceptions: Legal Duties**—person can be convicted for failure to act where legal duty to act. Common legal duties:
    a. **Statute**—where statute imposes duty.
    b. **Status**—where close "status relationship" exists.
    c. **Contract**—where contractual obligation exists.
    d. **Assumption of Duty**—where person takes initiative and performs act.
    e. **Creation of Peril**—where actor has created peril that confronts victim.
3. **Limitations on Legal Duties**—inapplicable where person is unaware of need to act, or does not have physical capacity to help.
4. *Lambert*—very limited defense excusing failures to act where legal duty when person not reasonably on notice that statute exists requiring action.

MENS REA

A. **The Basics**—showing of general wickedness not enough to establish mens rea.

1. **Mens Rea**—traditional name for mental state requirement.
2. **Sufficient Showing**—prosecution must prove specific mens rea element beyond a reasonable doubt.

3. **MPC Tests**—four levels of intentionality to be used as mens rea tests: purpose; knowledge; recklessness; and negligence.

   a. **Purpose**—accused's "conscious object" was to commit criminal act charged.

   b. **Knowledge**—accused was aware that nature of conduct was like that charged or was "practically certain" that it would cause criminal result.

   c. **Recklessness**—accused "consciously" disregarded substantial and unjustifiable risk of committing or causing criminal act which was "gross deviation" from what reasonable person would do.

   d. **Negligence**—accused "should" have been aware of substantial and unjustifiable risk of committing or causing criminal act which was "gross deviation" from what reasonable person would do.

   e. **Recklessness vs. Negligence**—for recklessness, accused has to actually be aware of risk of criminal conduct (subjective test), while for negligence, accused merely should have been aware (objective test).

4. **Concurrence of Act & Intent**—mens rea and actus reus must exist at same time to establish commission of crime.

5. **Modification of Elements**—mens rea element modifies other elements unless contrary legislative intent.

B. **Strict Liability**—most criminal offenses have mens rea element, but some do not.

1. **Common Law Origins**—if crime taken from common law contains no mens rea element, mens rea is still presumed to exist unless legislature states otherwise.

2. **Public Welfare Offenses**—if regulatory offense contains no mens rea element, it is strict liability if people are on notice that regulations of this sort exist, but not strict liability otherwise.

3. **Legislative Intention Controls**—legislature decides whether crime is strict liability or not; courts only interpret legislative intent.

C. **Intoxication & Drugged Condition**—mens rea defense in most jurisdictions if crime was specific intent, but not if general intent (or strict liability).

1. **General vs. Specific Intent**—general when conviction requires only proof of intent to commit act that causes the harm; specific when proof is required of an additional intent beyond committing act that causes the harm.

2. **Sufficiency**—intoxication or drugged condition must be so extreme that accused did not possess prescribed mens rea.

MISTAKE

A. **Mistake of Fact**—one way of negativing mens rea

1. **Depends on Mens Rea**—honest belief in mistaken circumstances must negative the particular mens rea of offense.

2. **Common Law Approach**—defense to specific intent crime when honest belief in mistake negativing mens rea; defense to general intent crime when honest and reasonable belief.

3. **MPC Approach**—elements of mistake defense depend upon particular mens rea element; reasonable mistaken belief required for recklessness and negligence.

4. **Strict Liability**—no mistake of fact defense.

5. **Jury Instructions**—mistake of fact may be covered in instruction on elements of crime charged.

B. **Mistake of Law**—not a defense.

1. **Distinguish Mistake of Fact**—mistake of fact defense relies on honest but mistaken belief in circumstances negativing mens rea; mistake of law is mistaken belief in lawfulness of conduct.

2. **Official Permission**—sometimes fact that accused was told officially that conduct was not criminal offense is good defense.

3. **Knowledge as Element**—good defense where legislature has made knowledge of illegality element of the crime.

CAUSATION

A. **Test**—two-pronged: actual (but for) causation + legal causation.

B. **Actual Causation**—but for the accused's actions, would criminal result have occurred when it did?

1. **Multiple Actors**—more than one person may be actual cause of same criminal result.

2. **Multiple Mortal Wounds**

a. **Simultaneous**—actual cause prong met by each actor if more than one independently inflict instantly fatal wounds on same victim at same time.

b. **Successive**—mixed law whether actual cause prong met where successive mortal wounds or wounds hastening death inflicted by independent actors.

C. **Legal Causation**—stricter test than tort law.

1. **Tests**—various names; focus on reasonable foreseeability and intervening or supervening causes that "break the causal chain."

2. **MPC**—was result "too remote or accidental"?

3. **Year and a Day Rule**—common law rule cutting off culpability after a year and a day largely rejected now.

4. **Medical Intervening Causes**—gross negligence breaks causal chain; ordinary negligence does not.

COMPLICITY

A. **Accomplice Liability**—guilt can be based upon helping someone else commit a crime.

1. **Common Law**—four categories of relationship to crime.

a. **Principal in the First Degree**—present and actually committed criminal act.

b. **Principal in the Second Degree**—present and assisted criminal act.

c. **Accessory Before the Fact**—aided or encouraged principals before crime completed.

d. **Accessory After the Fact**—aid or encouragement after crime completed.

e. **Shadowing**—accessory could not be convicted unless principal convicted.

2. **Merger**—principals and accessories merged today, except accessories after the fact.

   a. **Accessory Treated like Principal**—if prosecution proves assistance, accessory is guilty as if he or she was principal.

   b. **No Shadowing**—accessory can be convicted whether or not principal charged or convicted.

   c. **Notice**—prosecution must give notice whether it intends to prove accused acted as principal or accomplice.

   d. **Accessory After the Fact**—might be convicted of separate crime, but no merger with principal's offense.

3. **Mens Rea**—intent to assist another person in committing a crime, and intent that that person actually commit that crime.

   a. **No Direct Evidence**—mens rea often established circumstantially.

   b. **Mere Presence**—mere presence at scene of crime not enough for mens rea.

4. **Actus Reus**—active assistance of another in commission of crime.

   a. **Assisting Undercover Agent**—assisting undercover agent not criminal act.

   b. **Mere Presence**—mere presence at scene of crime not enough for actus reus.

5. **Renunciation or Withdrawal**—usually not a defense, but is defense in minority jurisdictions where before criminal act and actor keeps crime from occurring.

6. **Scope**—accused can be convicted for crimes intended to assist or could reasonably have foreseen.

7. ***Pinkerton* Doctrine**—conspirators held responsible for reasonably foreseeable actions of co-conspirators undertaken in furtherance of conspiracy.

B. **Vicarious Liability**—criminal conviction may be based upon another person's criminal conduct.

   1. **Corporate Responsibility**—where statute on point, corporations may be held responsible vicariously for actions of agents or employees.

2. **Corporate Officers**—corporate officers not usually held vicariously responsible for subordinates' criminal acts unless direct involvement.

3. **Powerlessness Defense**—no vicarious responsibility of corporate officers where no power to keep crime from occurring.

ATTEMPT

A. **Actus Reus**—beyond mere preparation.

   1. **Proximity Tests**—traditional tests focused on how close to crime person got.

   2. **Substantial Step Test**—MPC and majority test focuses on how far actor has gone toward crime.

   3. **Modern Test More Inclusive**—more actions beyond mere preparation are criminal attempts under modern test.

B. **Mens Rea**—intent to commit specific crime that was actor's objective.

   1. **Generalized Criminal Intent**—is not enough.

   2. **No Attempted Recklessness or Negligence Crimes**—attempting to cause a criminal result is intentional conduct.

C. **Merger**—attempt conviction merges with conviction for crime attempted.

D. **Abandonment Defense**—majority recognize attempt defense where person abandoned criminal objective before committing crime intended.

   1. **Voluntary**—not good defense if abandoned due to increased probability of detection or apprehension or greater difficulty.

   2. **Complete**—not good defense if only postponing conduct or switching target.

E. **Impossibility Defense**

   1. **Traditional Defense Existed**—only for legal impossibility; not for factual impossibility.

      a. **Factual Impossibility**—facts present, unknown to person acting, made commission of crime intended impossible.

b. **Legal Impossibility**—person committed acts which could not have amounted to crime charged as subject of attempt.

c. **Difference in Focus**—factual impossibility looked to what actor intended to do; legal impossibility looked to what actually occurred.

2. **MPC Rejects**—impossibility not a defense to attempt crimes today in many jurisdictions.

CONSPIRACY

A. **In General**—majority have conspiracy statutes, although controversial crime.

1. **Double Inchoates**—cannot conspire to attempt or solicit.

2. **Hearsay Exception**—hearsay statements of co-conspirators in furtherance of conspiracy may come into evidence.

B. **Unilateral or Bilateral Conspiracies**—unilateral approach is more inclusive.

1. **Bilateral**—traditional view: two or more persons must agree to commit unlawful act or lawful act by unlawful means.

a. ***Wharton's* Rule**—two people cannot be conspirators where they agree to commit crime that necessarily requires participation of both, unless more people involved.

b. **Undercover Agents**—cannot have conspiracy with undercover agent in bilateral jurisdiction.

2. **Unilateral**—now majority rule: one person may be conspirator if believes agreeing with another to commit crime.

a. **Undercover Agents**—can have conspiracy with undercover agent in unilateral jurisdiction.

b. **Co-Conspirator Status**—person is conspirator under unilateral approach even if co-conspirator is never found or identified, not charged, or acquitted.

C. **Mens Rea**—intent to agree with another to commit crime and intent to commit that crime.

1. **Recklessness & Negligence**—no conspiracy to commit crime with mens rea of recklessness or negligence.

2. **Mere Knowledge Not Enough**—mens rea not established simply by showing accused person knew someone else intended to commit crime.

D. **Actus Reus**—agreement with another person to commit crime (can be established circumstantially) plus, in many jurisdictions, overt act in furtherance of conspiracy.

1. **Number**—number of conspiracies is determined by number of agreements to commit crimes.

a. **Multiple Objectives**—one conspiratorial agreement may have multiple criminal objectives.

b. **Continuing Agreement**—conspiratorial agreement may continue over time.

2. **Merger**

a. **Conspiracy & Target Crime**—majority rule: conspiracy conviction does not merge with conviction for crime which was object of conspiracy.

b. **Multiple Inchoates**—convictions of multiple inchoates aimed at same target crime often do merge by statute.

E. **Overt Act**—act in furtherance of conspiracy by any conspirator; not the same as conspiratorial agreement.

F. **Duration**—abandonment of conspiracy presumed where no overt act within statutory limitations period.

G. **Renunciation & Withdrawal**—good defense to conspiracy in majority of jurisdictions.

1. **Voluntary**—withdrawal must be voluntary and not based on belief of increased risk of being caught by police.

2. **Complete**—withdrawal must be complete; cannot stop conspiring on one criminal objective while continuing another.

3. **Thwarting Crime**—person withdrawing must prevent commission of crime; can be accomplished by assisting police in preventing crime by co-conspirators.

H. **Scope of Conspiracies**—can conspire with unknown persons.

1. **Chains**—conspiracy where someone conspires with others up or down the line from him or her.

2. **Wheels & Spokes**—separate conspiracies (spokes) can be part of larger conspiracy where common co-conspirator

(hub) and conspirators knew of existence of other conspiracy or conspirators.

SOLICITATION

A. **In General**—majority have solicitation statutes, although controversial crime.

1. **General vs. Specific**—some statutes criminalize soliciting any crime; some only specific crimes.

2. **Accomplice**—if crime solicited occurs, solicitor is also accomplice.

B. **Mens Rea**—intent to promote or facilitate commission of specific crime by another person.

C. **Actus Reus**—commanding, encouraging, or requesting another person to commit specific crime.

1. **No Action Necessary**—neither party need act toward completing targeted crime.

2. **Not Mere Threats or Jokes**—must be more than that, but less than conspiratorial agreement.

3. **Mere Approval of Another's Criminal Intention Not Enough**—but can solicit by expressly encouraging person who has already decided to commit crime.

4. **Conspiracy**—if solicitation results in commission of crime by person solicited, conspiracy exists.

5. **Impossibility**—irrelevant what person being solicited did or whether crime solicited occurred.

D. **Renunciation and Withdrawal**—good defense to solicitation in some jurisdictions.

1. **Voluntary**—withdrawal must be voluntary and not based on belief of increased risk of being caught by police.

2. **Complete**—withdrawal must be complete; cannot abandon one criminal objective while continuing to solicit another.

3. **Preventing Crime**—person withdrawing must prevent commission of crime by person solicited.

ASSAULT

A. **Traditional Assault Crimes**—common law offenses.

1. **Battery**—intentional touching resulting in injury.

2. **Assault**—intentionally placing another in actual and reasonable fear of imminent battery.
    a. **No Touching Necessary**—includes acts intended only to scare another even if no physical contact, but verbal threats alone may not suffice.
    b. **No Real Danger Necessary**—victim's reasonable fear of battery enough.
    c. **Attempted Battery**—assault often treated as attempted battery.
    d. **Attempted Assault**—not a crime.

B. **Merger**—assault and battery elements commonly merged today into one simple assault crime.
1. **Combined Elements**—simple assault established by proof of either common law assault or battery.
2. **Simple Assault**—intentionally placing another person in fear of an imminent battery or intentionally committing a battery.

C. **Aggravated Assault**—wide variety of assault statutes punishing more severely assaults deemed to be more violent or serious.

SEX CRIMES

A. **In General**—sex crimes are assaults and/or batteries with a specified sexual element.
1. **Common Law Rape**—sexual intercourse by a male with a female not his wife, including vaginal penetration however slight, without consent and using force or threat of force.
2. **Common Law Evidentiary Requirements**—restrictions made rape difficult to prosecute and many victims and prosecutors unwilling to press charges.
    a. **Resistance**—victim needed to resist attack "to the utmost."
    b. **Corroboration**—corroborating evidence needed beyond victim's testimony.
    c. **Fresh Complaint**—victim needed to report attack quickly.
    d. **Impeachment**—evidence of victim's prior sexual conduct admissible to impeach victim's testimony.

3. **Modern Sex Crimes**—rape less difficult to prosecute today.
    a. **Changes from Common Law**
        i. **Elements**—common law elements eliminated or revised.
        ii. **Evidence**—requirements unique to rape cases eliminated or restricted.
        iii. **Rape-Shield Laws**—prevent introduction of irrelevant evidence of past sexual conduct.
        iv. **Gender Neutral**—apply to females as well as males.
    b. **Crimes Beyond Rape**—sexual assaults less serious than rape also criminalized.
    c. **Statute of Limitations**—rape prosecution barred after period of years but some movement to end such restrictions.

B. **Force**—common law element of rape.
1. **Modern Change**—often rape statutes require force or absence of consent, not both.
2. **Beyond Physical**—sometimes includes use of psychological pressure by accused as well as physical.
3. **Threat of Force**—may be verbal or non-verbal.
    a. **Serious Threats Only**—must be threat of death or serious physical harm to victim or another person.
    b. **Reasonable Fear**—victim's fear of force must be real and reasonable.
4. **Resistance**—victim no longer needs to resist but some jurisdictions define force by reference to overcoming victim's reasonable resistance.

C. **Absence of Consent**—common law element of rape.
1. **Modern Change**—often rape statutes require force or absence of consent, not both.
2. **Good Consent**—must be freely and voluntarily given by competent person.
    a. **Lack of Consent Need Not Be Verbal**—absence of consent can be inferred from actions.

b. **Not Coerced**—cannot be product of force, deception or duress.

c. **Not Impaired**—impaired victim not capable of good consent.

d. **Yes Can Change to No**—good consent may be withdrawn before or after intercourse has begun.

D. **Mens Rea**—traditionally treated like strict liability.

1. **Knowledge of Consent**—no need to prove accused knew or should have known that victim did not consent.

2. **Mistake**—in many jurisdictions, no defense that accused honestly and reasonably believed victim consented.

E. **Spousal Rape**—not a crime at common law.

1. **Modern Change**—common law abrogated.

a. **Immunity Eliminated**—same as rape in some states.

b. **Separate Crime**—separate spousal rape crime in some states, less serious than rape and fresh complaint requirement.

F. **Lesser Offenses**—more sex crimes than just rape today with less serious elements and punishments.

G. **Statutory Rape**—sexual intercourse with a minor below age of consent whether or not good consent or use of force.

1. **Mistake About Age Not a Defense**—minority permit defense of reasonable mistake of age within specified age range.

2. **Age Gap**—some jurisdictions require proof of specified age gap between accused and victim.

HOMICIDE

A. **In General**—specific homicide crimes vary widely by jurisdiction.

1. **Common Law**—murder and manslaughter.

a. **Murder**—killing another human being with "malice aforethought."

b. **Manslaughter**—killing another human being without "malice aforethought."

c. **Human Being**—not a fetus.

2. **Modern Homicide Crimes**—number of crimes, often separated by degrees.

3. **Elements**—killing act causing death of human being and specified mens rea.

B. **Murder**—need malice, express or implied.

1. **Malice Aforethought**—traditionally, wickedness of disposition, hardness of heart, wanton conduct, cruelty, recklessness of consequences, a mind without regard to social duty; legal term of art today.

   a. **Express**—proof of malicious thoughts or activity.

   b. **Implied**—implied from gross recklessness or extreme indifference to value of human life.

   c. **Presumption**—often presumed where use of deadly weapon on vital part of victim's body.

2. **First Degree**—also need premeditation and deliberation (p & d).

   a. **Intentional Killing**—specific intent to kill.

   b. **P & D**—actual prior thought and reflection.

      i. **Time**—key element.

         A. **Majority**—no time is too short.

         B. **Minority**—must be meaningful deliberation.

      ii. **Other Factors**—prior planning activity; prior relationship with victim; motive; and manner of killing.

3. **Second Degree**—malice without p & d.

4. **Felony Murder**—death occurring during felony or attempted felony.

   a. **Triggering Felony**—must prove all elements of specified felony.

      i. **Common List**—majority: list including robbery, rape, arson, burglary, and kidnapping.

      ii. **Dangerous Felonies**—minority: any dangerous felony.

      iii. **Independent Felony**—triggering felony must be independent of acts leading to victim's death.

      iv. **Res Gestae**—death must occur in proximity to and be caused by accused's acts.

b. **Killing by Accomplices**—some states: defense that unforeseeable killing by co-felon if accused not armed with deadly weapon.

c. **Killing by Others**—majority: not responsible for unforeseeable killing acts of others during felony.

d. **Responsive Killing**—responsible for death, including co-felon, resulting from response to accused's or accomplices' provocative acts.

e. **Flight After Felony**—still felony murder until felon has reached safe haven.

C. **Manslaughter**—killing without malice.

1. **Voluntary Manslaughter**—mitigated murder.

a. **Provocation Defense**—murder in the heat of passion.

i. **Elements**—sudden, intense passion resulting from provocation by victim so serious it would create passion in reasonable person.

ii. **Cooling-Off Period**—no defense where reasonable "cooling-off period."

iii. **Adequate Provocation**—common law: limited number of provocative acts; today, almost any act that would provoke reasonable person.

iv. **Reasonable Person**—consider circumstances as if in shoes of the defendant, but not extraordinary characteristics like hot temper.

v. **Words**—common law: words alone not enough to provoke; today: can be enough.

vi. **Wrong Victim**—defense applies where killing of someone else in attempt to kill provoker.

b. **Imperfect Defense**—traditional protective defense where belief in need to kill honest but unreasonable.

2. **Involuntary Manslaughter**—unintentional killing committed without malice.

a. **Mens Rea**—varies.

i. **Majority**—gross (criminal) negligence.

ii. **Minority**—recklessness or ordinary (civil) negligence.

3. **Misdemeanor Manslaughter**—largely abandoned.

D. **Negligent Homicide**—some states: separate negligence crime where involuntary manslaughter requires recklessness.

E. **Vehicular Homicide**—killing while accused driving and violating traffic law.

1. **Mens Rea**—varies: recklessness or negligence.

2. **Not Exclusive**—any homicide crime can apply to driver of vehicle.

THEFT

A. **Traditional Theft Crimes**—complicated and arcane elements.

1. **Larceny**—wrongful taking and carrying away of personal property in possession of another with intent to convert it or to deprive possessor of it permanently.

a. **Personal Property Only**—larceny inapplicable to real or intangible property, theft of services, or wild animals.

b. **Trespass on Possession**—larceny only applied to trespassing on possession of another.

i. **Not Custody**—not larceny to take property only in custody of another.

ii. **Custody Defined**—temporary control over property where right of use restricted legally by another.

c. **Breaking Bulk**—bailee taking all bailed goods not guilty of larceny; bailee taking only some bailed goods was "breaking bulk," and was guilty of larceny.

d. **Lost Property**—if clearly belonged to someone else, finder who took it, intending to keep it, was guilty of larceny.

i. **Return to Owner**—not larceny if finder intended to return it to owner.

ii. **No Clear Owner**—not larceny where not clear that lost property belonged to someone else.

e. **Asportation**—larceny requires movement "carrying away" beyond mere taking.

i. **Little Required**—movement even of inches sufficed.

- ii. **Today**—question is generally only whether control and dominion over property.
- f. **Mens Rea**—specific intent to convert or permanently deprive owner of property.
  - i. **Permanent**—includes unreasonably long period of time.
  - ii. **Return or Claim**—not larceny if reasonable intent to return property later or reasonable belief in claim to it.
- g. **Grand vs. Petty**—grand (serious) and petty (less serious) larceny distinguished usually by value of property taken.

2. **Larceny by Trick**—gaining possession of property from owner by fraud or false pretenses.
   - a. **Mens Rea**—intent to act fraudulently when property taken.
   - b. **Rentals**—treated differently.
     - i. **Older View**—not larceny by trick if person decided not to return property after it was taken.
     - ii. **Newer View**—failure to return rental property criminal.
3. **Embezzlement**—fraudulently converting property of another person while in lawful possession of it.
   - a. **Mens Rea**—specific intent; not crime if taker mistakenly believed owned it.
   - b. **Different from Larceny**—embezzlement when possessed property lawfully but then converted fraudulently; larceny when wrongfully took property in possession of another.
   - c. **Today**—theft by failure to make required disposition of funds: taking by person who obtained property subject to known obligation but used it for self instead.
4. **False Pretenses**—knowingly misrepresenting material facts to and with the result of defrauding another person into transferring title to his or her property.
   - a. **Mens Rea**—knowledge that representations were false, i.e. intent to defraud.

b. **Limited Misrepresentations**—does not include failure to disclose information or misrepresentations or exaggerations as to value of property.

c. **Different from Larceny by Trick**—false pretenses to fraudulently obtain title; larceny by trick to fraudulently obtain mere possession.

d. **Today**—false pretenses and larceny by trick often combined into theft by deception.

B. **Consolidation of Theft Offenses**—majority consolidate separate theft crimes into one inclusive theft offense.

1. **Variances in Evidence at Trial Okay**—theft established if prosecution for one included type of theft, but proof establishes different included type of theft.

2. **Grading**—punishment for different types of theft still different.

C. **Receiving Stolen Property**—gaining control over property believing it was obtained criminally, intending to permanently deprive owner of interest in it.

1. **Undercover Stings**—even if property not really stolen, still crime if accused believed it was; changed common law rule.

2. **Presumption**—knowledge that property stolen often presumed where person found in possession of stolen property from many people, prior receipt of such property, or dealer getting property he or she knows below reasonable value.

D. **Robbery**—theft with use or threat of violence or force.

1. **Common Law**—larceny with taking from or in presence of person accomplished by violence or threat of violence.

2. **Today**—theft where serious bodily injury inflicted or threatened, victim put in fear of such injury, or serious felony threatened.

E. **Burglary**—theft in a building.

1. **Common Law**—breaking and entering into another's dwelling at night with specific intent to commit a felony inside.

2. **Today**—entering a building or occupied structure intending to commit a crime inside.

a. **Time of Day**—irrelevant.

b. **License or Privilege**—not burglary where person licensed or privileged to enter premises.

JUSTIFICATION DEFENSES

A. **In General**—justification defenses permitted to allow otherwise unlawful response to certain external events.

1. **Justifications vs. Excuses**—justifications = external issues; excuses = internal issues.

2. **Affirmative Defenses**—most justification defenses are affirmative defenses.

a. **Relationship to Proof of Crime**—even if elements of crime proven, defendant may use affirmative defense by proving separate exculpatory elements.

b. **Burden of Proof**—usually preponderance of evidence not beyond a reasonable doubt.

B. **Self Defense**—commonly used in homicide prosecutions, but applies to other assaultive crimes as well.

1. **Test**—non-aggressor may use force to protect against attack by another person when reasonable belief threat of imminent use of force, and response is necessary to repel attack.

a. **Honest & Reasonable Belief**—subjective and objective elements.

i. **Subjective**—honest belief that there threat of force is imminent and use of responsive force necessary.

ii. **Objective**—belief that threat of force imminent and use of responsive force necessary must be reasonable.

iii. **Reasonable Person**—physical characteristics of accused may be considered, but not mental, emotional characteristics, or views.

b. **Necessity & Imminency**—threat of unlawful force must be imminent and response must be necessary.

i. **Relationship Between Elements**—imminency is one way to establish necessity; where no imminent danger, not necessary to act and defense inapplicable.

ii. **Battered Spouse Defense**—often no defense as no perceived imminency or necessity to act.

A. **Majority**—no defense.

B. **Experts**—some jurisdictions permit introduction of syndrome evidence: cycle of violence creates "learned helplessness."

c. **Aggressors**—not entitled to self defense.

i. **Test**—someone who threatens or initiates unlawful use of force.

ii. **Excessive Force**—if victim responds with excessive force, aggressor regains self defense right.

d. **Unlawful Arrest**—mixed law.

i. **Common Law** some jurisdictions retain common law rule that permits use of force to resist unlawful arrest.

ii. **MPC**—other jurisdictions follow MPC rule that no right to use force to resist unlawful arrest, unless excessive force being used.

e. **Deadly Force**—force intended or likely to cause death or serious bodily injury.

i. **Proportionality**—most jurisdictions follow MPC approach that use of deadly force okay only if threatened with deadly force.

ii. **Aggressors**—not entitled to use deadly force in self defense.

A. **Withdrawals**—aggressor regains self defense right if withdraws other than temporarily or strategically and makes withdrawal clear.

B. **Excessive Force**—if victim responds with to use of mere force with deadly force, aggressor regains self defense right.

iii. **Retreat Doctrine**—did not exist at common law.

A. **Scope**—many jurisdictions follow MPC approach that no right to use deadly force where person knows use can be avoided with complete safety by retreating.

B. **Castle Doctrine**—retreat doctrine inapplicable where person acting in own home, and sometimes place of work or beyond.

f. **Exception**—castle doctrine often inapplicable where person was initial aggressor or used force against co-habitant or co-worker.

g. **Battered Spouse**—in some jurisdictions, battered spouse does not need to retreat before using deadly force against abusing spouse.

C. **Defense of Others**—force used to defend against threat or attack on another person.

1. **Common Law**—unlike today, limited to defense of close relatives.

2. **Alter Ego Rule**—minority rule that right to act in defense of others limited by other person's right of self defense: "step into shoes" of victim.

3. **Today**—majority: defense of others okay if person reasonably believes use of force justified and necessary under circumstances.

4. **Retreat**—retreat doctrine inapplicable unless person using force and person being defended can both retreat in complete safety.

D. **Defense of Property or Habitation**—force used to defend real or personal property.

1. **Common Law**—depended on level of force used.

a. **Unlawful Force**—force could be used to protect property when reasonable belief immediately necessary.

b. **Deadly Force**—deadly force could be used only where reasonable belief necessary to prevent imminent, forcible entry into dwelling.

2. **Majority**—force can be used when reasonable belief necessary to prevent or terminate unlawful trespass or carrying away of property.

3. **Deadly Force**—deadly force can be used by a homeowner to prevent or terminate unlawful entry into dwelling when reasonable belief intruder intends to commit felony inside.

4. **Habitation**—some jurisdictions: deadly force permitted to terminate unlawful entry into person's dwelling where reasonable belief nothing less would terminate entry.

5. **Trap Guns**—not permitted.

E. **Imperfect Defenses**—mitigating defense in murder prosecution to voluntary manslaughter.

1. **Test**—accused honestly believed needed to use protective force but belief was unreasonable.

2. **Application**—not always permitted in recklessness or negligence crimes.

F. **Law Enforcement Defense**—force used to prevent crime or make an arrest.

1. **Common Law**—law enforcement officers could use reasonably necessary force to prevent or arrest for felony.

a **Misdemeanors**—non-deadly force only.

b. **Private Citizens**—depends on circumstances.

i. **Assisting Police**—same rights as officers.

ii. **Citizen's Arrest**—could only use force to arrest for felony.

2. **Majority**—depends on level of force used.

a. **Unlawful Force**—law enforcement officers can use force to prevent crime or make arrest when reasonably necessary.

b. **Deadly Force**—can be used only when reasonable belief substantial risk of serious danger if not used immediately.

G. **Necessity Defense**—commission of crime to prevent greater harm occurring from natural event.

1. **General Rule**—may commit crime when faced with imminent threat of serious injury and no reasonable and lawful alternative exists except commission of less serious crime to avoid threat.

2. **Recklessness or Negligence**—inapplicable to reckless or negligent crimes when person was reckless or negligent creating need to act.

3. **Homicide Excluded**—inapplicable to homicide charges.

4. **Objective Test**—was the criminal conduct reasonably necessary?

5. **Necessity vs. Duress**—necessity is response to natural events; duress is response to human threats.

H. **Consent of Victim**—valid defense only for some crimes.

EXCUSES

A. **In General**—excuses permitted as defenses because person's actions deemed not to be blameworthy.

1. **Excuses vs. Justifications**—excuses = internal issues; justifications = external issues.

2. **Affirmative Defenses**—many excuses are affirmative defenses.

a. **Relationship to Proof of Crime**—even if elements of crime proven, defendant may use affirmative defense by proving separate exculpatory elements.

b. **Burden of Proof**—usually preponderance of evidence not beyond a reasonable doubt.

B. **Duress**—excusable commission of crime due to coercion.

1. **General Rule**—may commit crime where reasonable belief of coercion by another with unlawful and imminent threat of death or serious bodily harm to actor or third party.

2. **Nature of Threat**—threat must be one reasonable person could not be expected to resist.

a. **Objective Test**—focus on actual coercion, not coerced person's belief.

b. **Threat to Third Parties**—majority rule; minority: only threats to close relatives.

3. **Recklessness or Negligence**—no duress where person recklessly or negligently placed self in probable duress situation.

4. **Homicide Excluded**—inapplicable to homicide charges.

5. **Prison Escapes**—sometimes additional requirement of good faith effort to turn self in after escape and duress ended.

6. **Duress vs. Necessity**—duress is response to human threats; necessity is response to natural events.

C. **Psychological Defenses**—no single approach required by Constitution.

1. **Insanity**—not guilty by reason of insanity (NGRI) verdict is complete defense.

   a. **Time of Crime**—insanity focus is time crime committed unlike competency focus on trial and ability to understand proceedings and participate in defense.

   b. **Post-NGRI**—discharge from criminal system but civil commitment proceedings.

   c. **Legal vs. Medical Tests**—insanity is legal term of art not medical.

   d. **Experts**—expert testimony can help jury decide if legal insanity test met.

   e. **Tests**—no one approach required and variety used.

      i. ***M'Naghten* Test**—traditional and most widely used: "A person is not responsible for criminal conduct if at the time of such conduct he was suffering from such a mental disease or defect as not to know the nature and quality of the act or, if he did know, that he did not know that what he was doing was wrong."

         A. **Cognitive Incapacity Prong**—"nature and quality" of act: focus on whether mental defect left accused unable to understand what he or she was doing.

         B. **Moral Incapacity Prong**—"did not know that what he was doing was wrong": focus on whether a mental disease or defect left accused unable to understand actions were wrong.

         C. **Irresistible Impulse**—in addition to *M'Naghten*, minority: also insane if acted on uncontrollable impulse rendering actor powerless to resist.

      ii. **MPC Test**—"[a] person is not responsible for criminal conduct if at the time of such conduct as a result of mental disease or defect he lacks substantial capacity either to appreciate the wrongfulness of his conduct or to conform his conduct to the requirements of law."

A. ***M'Naghten* Distinguished**—MPC test includes more types and degree of mental impairment.

B. **Hinckley Trial**—John Hinckley NGRI verdict in 1981 resulted in many jurisdictions dropping MPC test.

2. **Guilty But Mentally Ill**—minority: GBMI possible verdict for accused persons trying to get NGRI verdict.

a. **Insanity Distinguished**—GBMI test includes more types and degree of mental impairment than insanity test.

b. **Consequences**—different from NGRI.

i. **Criminal System**—no discharge from criminal system.

ii. **Sentencing**—sentenced as if guilty verdict.

iii. **Treatment**—right to treatment for mental illness.

iv. **Post-Cure**—returned to criminal system to complete sentence after recovery.

3. **Diminished Capacity**—accused did not have mental capacity to possess mens rea required for crime charged.

a. **Insanity Distinguished**—diminished capacity only negatives mens rea of certain crimes and is established with less serious showing of mental disorder.

b. **Consequences**—complete or mitigating defense for specific crimes, depending on jurisdiction.

D. **Entrapment**—defense where crime was product of police encouragement.

1. **Subjective Approach**—was accused predisposed to commit crime?

a. **Federal Test**—federal approach and approach in some states.

b. **Past Conduct**—character, reputation, and past criminal conduct relevant.

2. **Objective Approach**—how outrageous was the police conduct?

a. **MPC Test**—MPC approach and approach in some states.

b. **Past Conduct**—irrelevant.

3. **Mere Opportunity to Commit Crime**—not enough.

4. **Violent Crimes**—inapplicable.

E. **De Minimis Defense**—trivial charges may be dismissed by trial judge.